Professional competencies in language learning and teaching

Edited by Cecilia Goria, Lea Guetta, Neil Hughes, Sandra Reisenleutner, and Oranna Speicher

Published by Research-publishing.net, a not-for-profit association
Voillans, France, info@research-publishing.net

© 2019 by Editors (collective work)
© 2019 by Authors (individual work)

Professional competencies in language learning and teaching
Edited by Cecilia Goria, Lea Guetta, Neil Hughes, Sandra Reisenleutner, and Oranna Speicher

Publication date: 2019/06/08

Rights: the whole volume is published under the Attribution-NonCommercial-NoDerivatives International (CC BY-NC-ND) licence; **individual articles may have a different licence**. Under the CC BY-ND-ND licence, the volume is freely available online (https://doi.org/10.14705/rpnet.2019.34.9782490057399) for anybody to read, download, copy, and redistribute provided that the author(s), editorial team, and publisher are properly cited. Commercial use and derivative works are, however, not permitted.

Disclaimer: Research-publishing.net does not take any responsibility for the content of the pages written by the authors of this book. The authors have recognised that the work described was not published before, or that it was not under consideration for publication elsewhere. While the information in this book is believed to be true and accurate on the date of its going to press, neither the editorial team nor the publisher can accept any legal responsibility for any errors or omissions. The publisher makes no warranty, expressed or implied, with respect to the material contained herein. While Research-publishing.net is committed to publishing works of integrity, the words are the authors' alone.

Trademark notice: product or corporate names may be trademarks or registered trademarks, and are used only for identification and explanation without intent to infringe.

Copyrighted material: every effort has been made by the editorial team to trace copyright holders and to obtain their permission for the use of copyrighted material in this book. In the event of errors or omissions, please notify the publisher of any corrections that will need to be incorporated in future editions of this book.

Typeset by Research-publishing.net
Cover illustration by © j-mel - Adobe Stock.com
Cover design by © Raphaël Savina (raphael@savina.net)

ISBN13: 978-2-490057-39-9 (Ebook, PDF, colour)
ISBN13: 978-2-490057-40-5 (Ebook, EPUB, colour)
ISBN13: 978-2-490057-38-2 (Paperback - Print on demand, black and white)
Print on demand technology is a high-quality, innovative and ecological printing method; with which the book is never 'out of stock' or 'out of print'.

British Library Cataloguing-in-Publication Data.
A cataloguing record for this book is available from the British Library.

Legal deposit, UK: British Library.
Legal deposit, France: Bibliothèque Nationale de France - Dépôt légal: juin 2019.

Table of contents

v   Notes on contributors

1   Introduction
Cecilia Goria, Lea Guetta, Neil Hughes, Sandra Reisenleutner, and Oranna Speicher

9   Learning through teaching languages: the role of the teaching placement for undergraduate students
Tara Webster-Deakin

19   Enhancing learners' professional competence via Duolingo classroom
Billy Brick and Tiziana Cervi-Wilson

31   Enhancing independent learning competence and grammar language learning strategies
Jumana Ghannam

41   Training language professionals to be digitally proficient in an undergraduate and postgraduate context
María Jordano de la Torre

53   The EUniTA project: working with international partners to develop language, intercultural, and professional competencies in European university students
Sonia Cunico

65   Integrating the language aspects of intercultural competencies into language for specific purposes programmes
Zita Hajdu and Renáta Domonyi

77   Teaching intercultural competencies at the University of Debrecen
Ildikó Tar and Tímea Lázár

89   Intercultural competence in the language classroom
Marilena Minoia

99   Embedding employability in language learning: video CV in Spanish
Chelo de Andrés

Table of contents

111 Sharing the Year Abroad experience with non-language students: a student-led project on outward mobility
Anna de Berg

121 Can students be knowledge creators? A case study
Ruth Whittle

133 Beyond the language class
Mária Czellér and Klára Nagy-Bodnár

145 Author index

Notes on contributors

1. Editors

Dr Cecilia Goria is Associate Professor in the Department of Modern Languages and Cultures, University of Nottingham. She holds the role of Director Learning Director of the Faculty of Arts and is the Academic Leader of the distance learning Master's Degree in Digital Technologies for Language Teaching. Her interests are concerned with the design, principles, and practice of open learning, active learning, participatory pedagogies in online and blended teaching and learning.

Lea Guetta is Lecturer in Spanish in the Language Centre at the University of Nottingham. She is an experienced language teacher of both Spanish and French. Her teaching experience covers primary, secondary, sixth form, and the higher education sectors. She is also Director of Work-Related Learning in the School of Cultures, Languages, and Area Studies. She has a particular interest in preparing and supporting students for entering the world of work after university. With this in mind she has created The Work Placement & Employability programme for the School of Cultures, Languages, and Area Studies at the University of Nottingham.

Dr Neil Hughes is Director of Modern Language Teaching in the School of Cultures Languages and Area Studies and Digital Learning Director for the Faculty of Arts at the University of Nottingham. He has research interests in digital learning design, blended language learning, and Spanish politics (most recently on the issue of anti-tourism protests in Barcelona). He teaches at both undergraduate and postgraduate levels and delivers CPD training primarily in the area of blended learning design. He is also the academic lead for the Languages for Business initiative at the University of Nottingham that helps address the language and cultural needs of small and medium-sized enterprises in the East Midlands through student placements and workshops.

Sandra Reisenleutner is Assistant Professor at the University of Nottingham where she teaches German language and modules about language learning and teaching. Her research interests lie in the methodology and pedagogy of foreign

Notes on contributors

language learning and teaching. She has been working on a project fostering international collaboration on campus for the past few years.

Oranna Speicher is Associate Professor at the University of Nottingham where she currently serves as the Director of the Language Centre. She has been teaching German as a foreign language for over 20 years and her research interests are second language acquisition with a particular focus on technology-enhanced language learning and teaching as well as the role of the language teacher as teacher-researcher.

2. Reviewers

Caroline Campbell is School Assessment Lead and teaches EAP at the University of Leeds. With a background in language teaching, she is passionate about encouraging students to study languages and enabling them to articulate the value of their learning and the skills developed as a significant part of enhancing their employability. She is IWLP representative for the University Council of Modern Languages.

Dr Chiara Cirillo is Associate Professor in Second Language Education and the Director of the IWLP at the University of Reading. Her research background is in sociolinguistics, with a focus on gender and language. Over her twenty-year career in HE, she has taught Italian language and culture and developed an expertise in pedagogies in tertiary education. Her main areas of interest are assessment, intercultural competence, and teacher development. Dr Cirillo is Senior Fellow of the HEA and Executive Committee member of the Association of University Language Communities, the national body representing teaching and learning professionals in UK HEIs.

Sascha Stollhans is Senior Teaching Associate in German Studies at Lancaster University. His academic interests include (Germanic and Romance) languages and linguistics, second language acquisition, and language teaching pedagogy. His recent work has focussed on the role of languages in wider educational contexts and in educational policies, and he's currently co-leading a project to explore transitions and collaborations between different education sectors, funded by the "Language Acts and Worldmaking" strand of the AHRC Open World Research Initiative. Publications include a co-edited volume on "Innovative language teaching and learning at university: enhancing participation and collaboration", freely available at https://doi.org/10.14705/rpnet.2016.9781908416322.

3.   Reviewers/authors

Dr Chelo de Andrés is Associate Professor in Spanish Studies at Plymouth University, where she joined after having taught at Sheffield and Exeter Universities. Graduated from Universidad Complutense, Spain; she gained her PhD from The University of Sheffield. Enabling others to communicate in a second language remains the joy and pride of what she does. She has published articles, books, and reviews on Digital Tools for Language Learning. She has served as External Examiner and Chief Examiner for the Diploma of Spanish as a Foreign Language (DELE).

Billy Brick is Associate Professor in the School of Humanities at Coventry University. He is also Senior Fellow of the Higher Education Academy and a member of the Chartered Institute of Linguists. He teaches German language, materials and syllabus design in a multimedia world to undergraduate students, and computer assisted language learning at masters level and has been involved with numerous JISC/HEA projects including the Coventry Online Writing Lab (COWL) and the Humbox, an OER project for the humanities. He has published numerous articles in the field of technology and language learning, and his current research focus is in social media and language learning and evaluating mobile-assisted language learning apps.

Dr Sonia Cunico is the Director of Language Teaching for the Modern Languages degree programme and the Language Centre at the University of Exeter. She has taught Italian language and culture, translation studies, and

Notes on contributors

linguistics in a number of UK HE Institutions for over 25 years. She has a wide experience as a teacher trainer and has been involved in many national and international projects, such as the EU funded EUniTa project (European Universities Tandem Project). More recently, she has been interested in the role of intercultural competence in the modern languages degree and as part of the global citizenship agenda.

Dr Anna (Ania) de Berg is Senior Lecturer in German and International Mobility Coordinator at Sheffield Hallam University. Since 2001, she has been teaching languages and intercultural communication at several universities in Poland, Germany, and the UK. Her publications encompass a monograph on travel literature and a co-edited volume on visualisation of memory in Austrian media. Her main research interests lie in the field of internationalisation of higher education, global mobility, student experience, and the use of digital media in teaching.

Jumana Ghannam is Senior Lecturer at Nottingham Trent University and a Fellow of the Higher Education Academy. She is Subject Coordinator and Module Leader for the University Language Programme. Jumana has an MA in ELTD from the University of Nottingham, a postgraduate diploma in Teaching English Overseas, and a CELTA from Cambridge University. Jumana has been a leader, a trainer, and a coordinator for several courses in different universities and educational institutions in the Middle East and the UK. She is a qualified teacher trainer for teaching business from the University of South Carolina in the USA. Jumana is an occasional reviewer for some journals and books.

Marilena Minoia is Teaching Associate at the Language Centre, University of Nottingham, teaching French and Italian. Her role in the Language Centre also involves taking responsibilities of Widening Participation and outreach programmes, disability support, and extracurricular activities. Her main research interest lies in the implementation of intercultural awareness in foreign language teaching and learning and the use of technology to enhance collaboration and motivation in the classroom.

Notes on contributors

Tara Webster-Deakin is Widening Participation Manager and Teaching Associate at the University of Nottingham. She is in the process of writing up her doctorate in education, which explores the challenges to academic staff engaging in university outreach activities using participatory action research. Her teaching is rooted in education theory and practice and draws on her own experiences as a teacher in secondary education and an education manager in the charitable sector. Tara is an ardent advocate for social justice in education and a strong believer in inclusive practices.

Dr Ruth Whittle is Senior Lecturer in German Studies. In 2014 she was awarded a National Teaching Fellowship, which recognises 'excellent practice and outstanding achievement in learning and teaching in higher education' (HEA). Her latest book, with Sandra Salin, is Preparing Modern Languages Students for 'Difference'. Going beyond Graduate Skills (Peter Lang, 2017). She currently researches how students across different disciplines conceive of their learning journey. This is of particular interest to her in her role as the Senior Tutor of the School of Languages, Cultures, Art History, and Music.

4.   Authors

Tiziana Cervi-Wilson is Assistant Professor and the coordinator for the UWLP and career and employability modules for the English and Languages Department at Coventry University. She teaches all the Italian modules at all levels. She is Co-Project Leader for the Routes into Languages Project for the West Midlands Consortium at Coventry University. She is interested in language learning and teaching, digital literacy in language learning, multimedia, and computer assisted language learning. She has presented many joint papers investigating language learners' technology use inside and outside the classroom.

Mária Czellér PhD, is Associate Professor and Head of the Institute of Business Communication and Professional Language Studies at the University of

Notes on contributors

Debrecen, Hungary. Prior to this present position, she worked in France on a six-year bilateral contract as a visiting lecturer at the University of Strasbourg. Her academic interests include teaching languages for specific purposes.

Renáta Domonyi is Senior Language Teacher at the Institute of Business Communication and Professional Language Studies at the University of Debrecen, Hungary. Her academic interests include teaching languages (English and German) for specific purposes, methodology of teaching technical language, new approaches to vocabulary and skills development, curriculum development, and CLIL.

Zita Hajdu, PhD, is Assistant professor at the Institute of Business Communication and Professional Language Studies, the University of Debrecen, Hungary. She teaches English for Business and Economics and Translation for Business in the postgraduate economic technical translation course for MSc students. Her academic interests include intercultural studies, the relation between regional development and foreign language skills, technical translation, new methods in teaching grammar, and blended learning.

Dr María Jordano de la Torre works for the Department of Foreign Languages at the UNED (Universidad Nacional de Educación a Distancia) teaching and researching about ESP and CALL. She has been training teachers and language-related professionals in the field of ICT for two decades. She has participated in several research projects which dealt with the use of technology to teach languages. She belongs to the ATLAS research group.

Tímea Lázár is English Language Teacher at the Institute of Business Communication and Professional Language Studies at the Faculty of Economics and Business, University of Debrecen, Hungary, and a PhD student at the Károly Ihrig Doctoral School in Business Economics and Organisational Studies. Her academic interests include multicultural personality, intercultural competencies, employers' requirements for multicultural competencies, and intercultural communication studies.

Klára Nagy-Bodnár is Senior Language Teacher at the Institute of Business Communication and Professional Language Studies at the University of Debrecen, Hungary. Her academic interests include teaching languages for specific purposes, methodology of teaching technical language, new approaches to vocabulary and skills development, curriculum development, and technical translation.

Ildikó Tar, PhD, is Associate Professor and Vice Head of the Institute of Business Communication and Professional Language Studies at the University of Debrecen, Hungary. She is the Head of the postgraduate economic technical translation course for MSc students. Her academic interests include technical translation (English-Hungarian), legal English, psychology (coping with language anxiety for L2 learners of English), multicultural studies, and the use of CAT tools (MEMOQ) in translation.

Introduction

Cecilia Goria[1], Lea Guetta[2], Neil Hughes[3], Sandra Reisenleutner[4], and Oranna Speicher[5]

This volume examines many of the complex issues regarding the language skills and professional competencies acquired by students studying Modern Foreign Languages (MFL) at universities in the United Kingdom (UK) and across Europe. It also outlines the innovative pedagogical strategies, methods, and resources employed by language academics to help graduates to transition from university into the world of work through their MFL studies. The chapters it comprises are based on extensive enquiries, discussions, and practice on the part of the authors, and offer a wealth of thought-provoking ideas and examples that readers can reflect upon and integrate successfully into their own teaching practice. These issues were discussed at the Professional Competencies in Language Learning and Teaching that took place on the 12th-13th of July 2018 at the University of Nottingham. The conference that was organised as a collaboration between The Department of Modern Languages and Cultures and the Confucius Institute of the University of Nottingham brought together researchers, practitioners, employers, and experts working on the relation between 21st century professional competencies and language education. This introduction to the volume provides some of the wider context within which the initiatives addressed by the authors are situated and sets out the broad themes they discuss.

Whilst the main disciplinary focus of the conference was MFL, several authors begin their chapters with the claim that the question of employability and higher

---

1. University of Nottingham, Nottingham, England; cecilia.goria@nottingham.ac.uk
2. University of Nottingham, Nottingham, England; lea.guetta@nottingham.ac.uk
3. University of Nottingham, Nottingham, England; neil.hughes@nottingham.ac.uk; https://orcid.org/0000-0002-0617-316X
4. University of Nottingham, Nottingham, England; sandra.reisenleutner@nottingham.ac.uk
5. University of Nottingham, Nottingham, England; oranna.speicher@nottingham.ac.uk

How to cite: Goria, C., Guetta, L., Hughes, N., Reisenleutner, S., & Speicher, O. (2019). Introduction. In C. Goria, L. Guetta, N. Hughes, S. Reisenleutner & O. Speicher (Eds), *Professional competencies in language learning and teaching* (pp. 1-8). Research-publishing.net. https://doi.org/10.14705/rpnet.2019.34.909

Introduction

education's contribution to it is an issue for the sector as a whole, not just languages. **Webster-Deakin** in Chapter 1, for example, points towards the debate that has been raging for some time in the UK about the extent to which university courses are equipping their students with the hard and soft skills, knowledge, and competencies necessary for both successful and fulfilling careers and to meet the needs of businesses and of society more widely. It should come as no surprise therefore that such discussions have been the catalyst for a growing number of articles, papers, frameworks, and conferences seeking to draw attention to 21st century professional competencies and how universities might integrate a focus on these into their curriculum. In the context of the UK, arguably the most influential document in this area is the Higher Education Academy's (HEA) Embedding Employability Framework that, as Webster-Deakin argues, offers a structure and process for developing ways in which to deliver these skills across the higher education sector. According to the HEA, providers within the sector are coming under increasing pressure from all stakeholders including alumni, employers, government bodies, parents, and professional organisations, not to mention their current students, to prioritise this agenda in their strategic planning processes and arrangements. As **Brick** and **Cervi-Wilson** argue in Chapter 2 of this volume, one institution where the HEA framework has been influential is the University of Coventry. As they explain in their contribution, Coventry has taken considerable steps to develop strategies that "emphasise and stress the importance of education for employability" in a wide range of contexts including in the university's institution-wide language programme.

As with the University of Coventry initiative and the high levels of interest this conference attracted from both the UK and across the world, debates about employability are also very much to the fore in MFL. Interestingly, much of the most insightful work has been led by organisations outside higher education by the likes of the Confederation of British Industry and the British Council. In both cases, these important bodies have sought to establish the value of languages education to the economy and society more broadly and to use such evidence in efforts to arrest the decline in language teaching and learning that has taken place across all sectors of education and strengthen the case for funding despite falling recruitment onto language programmes and courses. As Bernadette Holmes explained in her keynote address to the conference, since at least 2010, there has been an ever-growing chorus lamenting the falling numbers of UK graduates with high level language skills and the impact this is having on the UK economy.

Holmes, who has been leading the *Born Global* project for the British Academy (https://www.thebritishacademy.ac.uk/born-global), emphasised the extent to which modern workplaces, not just in transnational corporations but also in the case of Small and Medium sized Enterprises (SMEs), need their employees to be able to speak more than one language if they are going to compete effectively in the global marketplace. As she explained, employers are increasingly of the belief that languages add value to their businesses, both internally and externally, to help build and sustain collaborative networks within multilingual and culturally diverse workplaces and help strengthen existing and develop new client relationships by building rapport and developing trust. As she points out elsewhere (Holmes, 2016), "when clients come from a different language community, if a company can connect using a common language, this adds to their credibility and to their competitive advantage. Contracts can be won or lost on an organisation's ability to speak the client's language and understand a client's culture" (p.184).

Holmes is particularly interested in the impact the language skills deficit is having on SMEs. As she reported in her keynote, in its 2013 report, *Roads to Success: SME Exports,* the Select Committee on SMEs of the UK House of Lords stated that "there are significant commercial benefits (to SMEs) to addressing the language issue and adverse consequences if it is ignored" (House of Lords, 2013, p. 60). The report found evidence to support claims around the link between language skills and business performance. Thus, some 18% of SMEs in the UK see a lack of language skills and cultural knowledge as a barrier to exporting. Research carried out by Gregory and Hughes (2018) at the University of Nottingham also corroborates these findings. A survey they carried out with local SMEs identified a number of issues including a marked over-reliance on English as a medium of communication in international trade. Out of the total number of instances that an important foreign market was named by a given business in the survey, English was identified as the language used to conduct international trade in

Introduction

64% of them. The reliance on English as the primary means of communication was particularly apparent in the context of customer service delivery, where only 4% of the companies surveyed reported usage of languages other than English. The survey results also provided evidence to corroborate the view that business is being lost because of the UK's lack of foreign language skills. Thus, 16% of the companies surveyed felt that they have or may have lost opportunities to win contracts due to a lack of linguistic and cultural competence. One of the reasons for the relatively poor overseas trading performance of companies taking part in the survey is the absence of a management strategy to address their language and cultural deficits. Of the companies surveyed, 80% stated that there was no such strategy in place.

One of the other main themes of the volume is the skills and knowledge acquired through language study that go beyond mere proficiency in the target language. Included here are many of the social skills, character traits, and employment qualities that make up the soft skills that are so highly valued, but so often lacking, in the workforce such as teamwork, problem-solving, confidence, resilience, independence, cross-culturality, problem-solving, and action planning. The ways in which such skills are developed, often incidentally, within higher education language courses was a theme picked up by several authors. For example, **Ghannam** in Chapter 3 seeks to establish the link between the deductive and inductive teaching of explicit grammatical knowledge and the development of key employability skills in areas such as strategic thinking and the type of autonomy seen by most employers as crucial in building employee engagement and to be a key ingredient in innovation. **Jordano de la Torre** in Chapter 4, on the other hand, explains the affordances of the modern language classroom for delivering key digital competencies such as online literacy and digital content creation. She explores these themes in her own context of teaching, the Spanish National University of Distance Learning in which, due to the remoteness, heterogeneity, and flexible learning needs of students, technology plays a central role in delivery.

The use of digital technologies in language teaching and the contribution they make to supporting student employability also comes up elsewhere in the volume. As reported by **Cunico** in Chapter 5, the University of Exeter is exploiting the affordances of digital technology in the European-funded EUnita project to create an online tandem platform that provides opportunities for learners' social interactions with native speakers across Europe. In addition to promoting language learning, EUnita emphasises the skills students acquire indirectly as a result of taking part in tandem partnerships in areas such as communication, autonomy, reciprocity, and intercultural learning. Brick and Cervi-Wilson in Chapter 2 also focus on technology in their study on the uses and impact of Duolingo, not just in terms of language acquisition, but also in relation to the types of general employability and digital competencies it promotes. This is likely to be a crucial area of focus for languages in the future, particularly given the emergence of what is being described as the fourth industrial revolution, leading to the appearance of new and formerly unseen economic sectors in which digital content creation, digital literacy, artificial intelligence, and big data analysis are to the fore. In the UK alone, the growth rate of the businesses within the digital sector is more than twice that of the UK business sector as a whole.

The issue of intercultural communication and its importance for employability is a key theme running through several of the authors' works. In Chapter 6, for example, **Hajdu** and **Domonyi**, report on the efforts the Institute of Business Communication and Professional Language Studies at the Debrecen University in Hungary have made to incorporate intercultural competence into courses at both undergraduate and postgraduate levels, and the important role this is playing in helping students transition from university into the world of work. This reflects the Institute's belief that such awareness and sensitivity shapes employees' ability to work effectively in the increasingly multicultural and multilingual teams found in many of the world's major organisations. In their contribution, they explore the complex affective, cognitive, and behavioural aspects at play in intercultural communication and explain the steps they have taken to ensure their courses integrate a focus on these in an effort to prepare their students "for the challenges of the future labour market". **Tar** and **Lázár** in Chapter 7 also look at this issue from a Hungarian perspective in their report on the intercultural awareness of students enrolled at the Budapest College of

Introduction

Communication, Business, and Arts. In contrast, **Minoia** in Chapter 8 sets out the practical approach based on Deardorff's (2006) intercultural competence model that she uses to address similar dimensions of intercultural competence with Chinese students from the University of Nottingham's Ningbo campus on international exchange in Nottingham.

As with Minoia, the pedagogical implications of a greater focus on generic employability skills and competencies, within the context of language teaching, loom large in the contributions of several other authors. The range of methodologies and approaches suggested are reflective of their diverse origins and academic backgrounds. In all cases, the accurate descriptions of pedagogical practice help readers replicate the approach within their own context of language teaching and learning. In her chapter on her video CV project for students of Spanish, for example, **De Andrés** in Chapter 9 provides a step-by-step guide looking at how, over a six-week period, she develops her learners' ability to write scripts and produce videos in Spanish in which they articulate their personal qualities and describe their achievements and the value of these for employability purposes.

At the University of Nottingham, where the conference that constitutes the catalyst for this volume was held, languages academics have explored a number of ways of addressing employability skills, including by integrating them into the curriculum and by offering students exciting opportunities to avail themselves of workplace opportunities both during their year abroad and whilst studying in the UK. Within the School of Cultures, Languages, and Area Studies, for example, the *Work Placements and Employability Programme,* led by Lea Guetta, provides students with the opportunity to gain first hand practical experience and to meet and network with a wide range of employers. This is also the focus of the *Languages for Business* initiative that works specifically with SMEs in the East Midlands. The important role that placements and work-based training play in the MFL context at the University of Nottingham is discussed by Tara Webster-Deakin in Chapter 1. In it, she explains the opportunities the delivery of her Undergraduate Ambassador Scheme module provides to final year language students contemplating a professional career in MFL. According to Webster-

Deakin, the most challenging aspect of the modules is the period of teaching practice that participating students undertake within schools. The module also incorporates classes on effective teaching practice, language learning theory, activity design, and the role of digital technologies in language teaching and learning.

The work experience theme is also explored in **De Berg**'s contribution Chapter 10 and, to a certain extent, in **Whittle**'s Chapter 11. In it, she explores ways in which students can engage "with the knowledge and skills they need to become independent problem-solvers and natural leaders" through a process of critical evaluation and knowledge creation within the context of a module she delivers at the University of Birmingham. In *Sex, Submission, and Seduction,* students of German become partners in "research and inquiry" as they explore, through the medium of both English and German, key features of the module design and delivery. De Berg, on the other hand, explores a number of relevant questions in areas such as internationalisation, intercultural competence, and student mobility in her study of a project designed to increase student international mobility at the Sheffield Business School at Sheffield Hallam University. As part of their contribution to the project, students studying on the Language with International Business, Marketing, and Tourism programme are tasked with building a strategy to increase awareness and uptake of international mobility opportunities among students on non-language degree programmes.

Finally, whilst the main focus of the volume is the acquisition of transferable employability skills through the medium of foreign language teaching, the value of language skills per se and the importance of these for the employability prospects of both specialist learners studying on named modern foreign language degrees and non-specialist learners taking supplementary courses in languages is addressed in the volume. For example, **Czellér** and **Nagy-Bodnár** in Chapter 12, highlight the importance of learning languages for specific purposes such as for work and business. They argue for strategies that support students to develop a language (English in their case) register appropriate to the business context they will be working in characterised by, in particular, specialist lexical items and complex grammatical features.

Introduction

References

Deardorff, D. K. (2006). Identification and assessment of intercultural competence as a student outcome of internationalization. *Journal of Studies in International Education, 10*(3), 241-266. https://doi.org/10.1177/1028315306287002

Gregory, J., & Hughes, N. (2018). *Building capital through student placements: the case of languages for business.* http://www.asetonline.org/wp-content/uploads/2018/11/2018-Proceedings.pdf

Higher Education Academy. (2016). *Embedding employability framework.* https://www.heacademy.ac.uk/system/files/downloads/embedding-employability-in-he.pdf

Holmes, B. (2016). In focus... The age of the monolingual has passed: multilingualism is the new normal. In E. Corradini, K. Borthwick & A. Gallagher-Brett (Eds), *Employability for languages: a handbook* (pp. 181-188). https://doi.org/10.14705/rpnet.2016.cbg2016.481

House of Lords. (2013). *Select committee on small and medium sized enterprises of the UK House of Lords, roads to success: SME exports.* Authority of the House of Lords. https://publications.parliament.uk/pa/ld201213/ldselect/ldsmall/131/131.pdf

1. Learning through teaching languages: the role of the teaching placement for undergraduate students

Tara Webster-Deakin[1]

Abstract

The Higher Education Academy (HEA) Embedding Employability framework lists a broad range of employability skills they have identified as being imperative to graduate success in the workplace, including "knowledge and application, self, social and cultural awareness and reflection and articulation" (HEA, 2015, diagram, n.p.). The final year Undergraduate Ambassador Scheme (UAS) module in the School of Cultures, Languages, and Area Studies, 'Communicating and Teaching Languages', delivers the majority of these skills identified as necessary for graduate employability while combining the acquisition of these with rigorous academic student outputs. While teaching as a career is not for everyone, the module provides an opportunity for final year linguists to apply their knowledge in a real-world context and offers them a testing ground for their own language skills and competencies as well as the chance to position themselves as adults in a work environment. In local inner city and county schools, they learn about the complexities of professional relationships, curriculum constraints, political agendas, and home-school relationships while constructing and evaluating lesson plans for a range of learning needs. Supported by seminars delivered by an educationalist, the experience of the students-as-teachers can be seen to follow the same plan-act-observe-reflect cycle as is commonly used in teacher action research (Elliott, 1985; Schön, 1987). As

---

1. University of Nottingham, Nottingham, England; afztw@exmail.nottingham.ac.uk

How to cite this chapter: Webster-Deakin, T. (2019). Learning through teaching languages: the role of the teaching placement for undergraduate students. In C. Goria, L. Guetta, N. Hughes, S. Reisenleutner & O. Speicher (Eds), *Professional competencies in language learning and teaching* (pp. 9-18). Research-publishing.net. https://doi.org/10.14705/rpnet.2019.34.910

with professional teacher action research, students are required to demonstrate "a willingness to learn about their own classrooms and a desire to develop themselves professionally" (Nixon, 1981, p. 9). This article outlines the composition of the UAS programme, its challenges, and the opportunity it provides for final year linguists to develop a range of professional competencies for their future careers.

Keywords: action research, teaching, undergraduates, languages, reflective learning.

1. Introduction

One of the challenges that universities in the UK face is how to successfully provide meaningful opportunities for developing employability skills while ensuring academic study retains its rigour and its criticality. The HEA Embedding Employability framework (HEA, 2015, n.p.) offers a structure for developing ways in which to deliver these skills in higher education. The framework lists those employability skills they believe to be significant assets to graduate success in the workplace such as knowledge, cultural awareness, and self-reflection (HEA, 2015). Typically, universities offer a range of extra-curricular, or, in some cases, credit-bearing career-focussed modules including internships, work experiences, and industry placements. These can be helpful in developing students' skills and attributes alongside their knowledge and, in some cases, their evolving identity as a citizen (Artess, Mellors-Bourne, & Hooley, 2017).

As a teaching associate who teaches cohorts of final year undergraduate students of languages, I have had the opportunity to develop and refine a module which can be said to go some way towards addressing the complex issue of developing the professional competencies the HEA suggests universities might consider when designing and delivering the curriculum. Originally conceived for Science, Technology, Engineering, and Mathematics (STEM) subjects in higher education institutions in order to respond to the growing deficit in science and mathematics teachers, the UAS offers a threefold opportunity to undergraduate students, subject teachers in local schools, and the pupils attending those schools. More recently, this scheme or academic module has been re-imagined for languages undergraduates, many of whom are considering entering the teaching profession following their positive experience of teaching English during their study year abroad.

UAS is a model which has run successfully in nearly 60 UK universities since 2003, although the languages model is less common and responds to a more recent, concerning deficit of language teachers entering the profession with the resulting negative impact on the take-up of languages at General Certificate of Secondary Education (GCSE) and above. In 2016/2017, only 50% of GCSE candidates sat a language examination, and only 33% of these achieved a C grade or above. The data for A level uptake and success also show a deficit, and this has resulted in a lack of suitably qualified teachers in secondary and a negligible number of primary teachers having the requisite level and confidence in languages to teach the required basic skills to their junior pupils (Tinsley & Board, 2016).

2. The UAS programme – application, allocation, and curriculum

Participation in the module involves engaging in a varied and, at times, demanding set of activities and endeavours, collectively and individually. Students sometimes feel overwhelmed in the first few weeks when they are required to balance obtaining an enhanced disclosure and barring service check while summarising their teaching philosophy and completing their 'availability to teach' form alongside attending the seminar. While support is provided, I am careful to accentuate the necessity for multi-tasking in anticipation of their teaching practice. Access to the module is by application as the places are limited due to the availability of teaching placements. The application, although not particularly onerous, is the first in several hurdles which aim to situate the learning in a real-world context. The module is regularly over-subscribed, with 40+ languages students applying for the 25-30 available places.

Chapter 1

Once the students are enrolled, the module runs for the full academic year, providing the participants with 20 academic credits and a total mark which contributes to their final degree classification. A weekly seminar runs throughout the year, including topics such as classroom management, learning theory, the pastoral role, assessment, and technology in language learning (see supplementary material). The curriculum was constructed in consultation with the university's Postgraduate Certificate in Education (PGCE) Modern Foreign Languages (MFL) team, and annual feedback from local teachers provides appropriate updates to this. In addition, an MFL secondary school teacher delivers one of the seminars on language learning theory each year, to bring current practice directly from her classroom to the students. Assessment is in two parts; a 1,000 word lesson plan (25% of the final mark) and a 3,000 word critically reflective essay (75% of the final mark). These are submitted at the end of the first semester (lesson plan) and the second semester (essay).

The style of the seminar aims to demonstrate effective classroom practice; varied learning activities and groupings, a platform for student to voice their opinions, and ongoing opportunities to reflect on and share their teaching experiences. Module teaching is underpinned by relevant and current educational theory and practice, and encourages the students to pursue their own academic reading in an area that becomes of significant interest to them during their placement. This occurs in the second semester, is hosted by local school languages departments, and offers each student the individual opportunity to teach six lessons to a group or class of pupils.

Sourcing and maintaining the teaching placements requires a large amount of time and effort, both to recruit schools to the programme and to ensure the introduction of the students is a smooth and positive process. In the case of the former, there can be a last minute plea via email to schools who have offered a single placement to provide multiple placements where there is a dearth of teaching opportunities for German, for instance. Invariably, these pleas produce the requisite placements, mainly due to well-established relationships with placement schools nurtured over several years. In the case of the latter, expectations of both the placement school and the student are articulated in class at an introductory placement teacher and student meeting and via email. As module convenor, I have to offer support to dissatisfied teachers and forgetful students in the form of reminders, follow-up telephone calls, thank you cards, and emails. The cohort of primary and secondary schools has steadily increased, and schools tend to return to offer placements year on year. Teachers cite as advantages the positive language learning role models the students present to their pupils, as well as the extra support for oral, grammar, and beginners' language learning.

3. Development of professional competencies

Much of what is expected of the students participating on the module and what they instinctively start to develop can be aligned to many elements in the HEA Embedding Employability framework: knowledge and application; reflection and articulation; self, social, and cultural awareness; and confidence, resilience, and adaptability. Evidence for this can be found in their teaching journals which they maintain throughout the module and in which they write up their reflections on meeting their placement contact teacher or class for the first time, as well as evaluating each lesson and planning for the subsequent one. This journal not only provides the qualitative evidence for their final assessed essay, it also charts their experience as novice language teachers and documents their challenges and successes.

While the practical classroom experience is useful for the aspiring language teachers in each cohort, it is the critical reflection on this which provides the self-knowledge needed for success in the future workplace and as a global citizen. Knight and Yorke (2003) determine employability in higher education to mean knowledge, attributes, and skills *plus*. The *plus* is comprised of

> "self-theories (how we explain what we experience), locus of control (whether we think we are generally able to affect our experiences) and their motivational concomitants (whether we therefore strive, comply or resist)" (Knight & Yorke, 2003, p. 7).

The definition of *plus* can be seen to provide a narrative of the UAS student experience as they navigate their path through teaching grammar or vocabulary in unfamiliar and sometimes confrontational learning settings. Conceptually, they learn what they can and cannot control about their teaching context, and how they can influence this. Practically, the students learn how to survive a less than successful lesson, regroup, and return with new and reflective strategies for classroom success. Academically, they find the synergy between their experience and the critical evaluation they need to employ to write their assignment. The module as a whole requires them to be responsive, resilient, and reflective, three of the qualities that help the students in the classroom, and in their final assignment. Reflecting on the three elements of the *plus*, I created a model (Figure 1 below) which encapsulates the requirements of the final year students in their teaching placement and the challenges therein.

Figure 1. Reflective, Reflexive and responsive, Agile, Adaptable, and Prepared (RRAAP) model

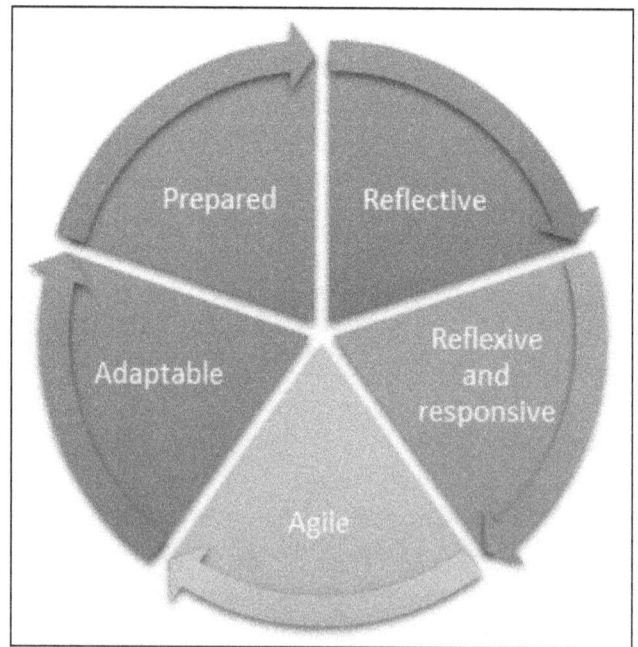

The module requires the students to be reflective learners in order to evaluate and adjust their teaching plan, style, or approach for the following week. They are required to prepare for every conceivable classroom eventuality of pupil behaviour and range of pupil ability. It asks them to be reflexive and responsive so that they are aware of themselves and their actions in relation to the pupils and able to respond to the needs of the classroom in the teaching moment. It also requires them to be agile in their ability to move fluidly between the roles of student (learner) and teacher; something which is neither intuitive nor easy to achieve. Students are also expected to be adaptable to the demands, boundaries, and customs of an unfamiliar school environment and prepared to foster collegiate relationships with the teachers and yet, at the same time, authoritative ones with the pupils in the school.

4. Links to educational action research

The competencies as outlined in the model above are in line with the principles of educational action research (Elliott, 1985; Schön, 1987). This positions the teacher as a researcher of their classroom in which they teach, reflect on, and improve their practice, thus ensuring that classroom pedagogy has a critical evidence base. The research process is an iterative one, providing ongoing opportunities for reflection and re-positioning of the teacher and her planning and delivery. In action research, the notion of 'mess' is a common one as researchers change direction and move backwards as well as forwards as they make sense of the actions they have taken (Cook, 2009). This mess and the resolution thereof reflect the complexities of a working environment.

The undertakings of the language undergraduates can be seen to emulate the action research cycle of plan-act-observe-reflect (Carr & Kemmis, 1986), following a recognisable pedagogical process using lesson evaluation and reflection to alter or re-think the subsequent lesson in the light of the lesson outcomes, responses, and levels of engagement. The students' abilities to assess, make a judgement, and implement a change are high level competencies relevant to all places of work and crucial to strategic change processes and operational management as well as outstanding lessons. While only a proportion of the students each year continue on to become teachers, the experience of applying their linguistic knowledge to a real-life and sometimes challenging context is advantageous to all in preparing for and securing their future roles.

5. Conclusion

It would be neither fair nor accurate to imply that the teaching placements and the intersection of student schedules and priorities with the pressures and challenges of schools is without its difficulties. For the school staff, they are required to support a novice and often-nervous undergraduate while continuing to deliver the curriculum and manage their own teaching load. For the students, there are many challenges. Different teaching groups week on week, last minute changes, a lack of clear guidance, and sparse communication from their contact teacher are a few of the regular barriers faced by the students as they prepare themselves to teach. Yet it is the ability of the students to navigate their way through which provides a visible arc of their development as professionals and as adults, not simply as academic products. Nixon (1981), in his work on educational action research, described what was required of the teacher-researcher as "a willingness on the part of the teachers to learn about their classrooms and a desire to develop themselves professionally" (p. 9).

The agility required to balance the dual role of teacher and learner together with the humility required to evaluate their teaching practice places high demands on the participating students but also yields very positive results. The complexities with which the students grapple and the sophistication of their responses demonstrate their 'willingness' to self-develop as future teachers and professionals. Their experiences on this module can be understood through their voices via excerpts from their reflective final assignments and comments in their module evaluation forms:

> "Understanding language anxiety became a crucial element of my teaching experience as it affected most of my students".

"I have deduced through my experiences that it is important for a teacher to view a class not as a homogeneous unit, but rather a group of individuals with varying abilities caused by different needs, learning preferences, and circumstances".

"This module was extremely relevant to the career path I plan to take after university. I feel very well equipped with both theoretical knowledge and practical experience from this module".

"The module ran very smoothly across the year and also in a logical way. The methods of assessment are particularly useful for students who want to go on and become teachers".

The undergraduate students have a key role to play in learning from their teaching experience, acting as change agents throughout the process and benefiting their own praxis development and the development of the pupils they teach. The benefits of the additional workload such a module entails are in the marriage between academic study and real-world teaching experience. This does not dilute the academic requirements but rather adds to them through careful and thoughtful observation and reflection. It enables deep engagement with the literatures to draw informed, evidence-based conclusions based on each student's direct experience.

Supplementary materials

https://research-publishing.box.com/s/i15q67693vval1dslectp8h937vs2k8r

References

Artess, J., Mellors-Bourne, R., & Hooley, T. (2017). Employability: a review of the literature 2012-2016. Higher Education Academy. https://derby.openrepository.com/handle/10545/621285

Carr, W., & Kemmis, S. (1986). *Becoming critical: education, knowledge and action research.* Falmer.

Cook, T. (2009). The purpose of mess in action research: building rigour though a messy turn. *Educational Action Research, 17*(2), 277-291. https://doi.org/10.1080/09650790902914241

Elliott, J. (1985). *Educational Action-Research.* Opinion Paper.

HEA. (2015). *Framework for embedding employability in higher education.* https://www.heacademy.ac.uk/knowledge-hub/framework-embedding-employability-higher-education

Knight, P. T., & Yorke, M. (2003). Employability and good learning in higher education. *Teaching in Higher education, 8*(1), 3-16. https://doi.org/10.1080/1356251032000052294

Nixon, J. (1981). *A teacher's guide to action research.* Grant McIntyre.

Schön, D. A. (1987). *Educating the reflective practitioner.* Jossey-Bass.

Tinsley, T., & Board, K. (2016). *Language trends 2015/16: the state of language learning in primary and secondary schools in england: report.* Education Development Trust.

2. Enhancing learners' professional competence via Duolingo classroom

Billy Brick[1] and Tiziana Cervi-Wilson[2]

Abstract

Coventry University Institution Wide Language Programme (IWLP) offers beginners language learning modules to approximately 3,000 students. Each module is taught over 11 weeks for a total of one hour and 40 minutes and two of the weeks are used for in class tests, so tutors generally agree that students need to practise their skills outside the classroom in order to pass the module. One way of doing this was to use the language learning app, Duolingo, which helps students to gradually broaden their linguistic, professional competence, and digital fluency through increased learner autonomy. How effective this approach is, however, has never been measured. The project ran from January to April 2018 and explored whether a correlation exists between regular use of the app by IWLP learners at Common European Framework of Reference (CEFR) level A1 of French, German, Italian, Portuguese, and Spanish, and achieving a high formal coursework assessment mark. The views of both learners and tutors of their experiences of using the software, and the tutor tools provided by Duolingo Schools, will also be canvassed. A virtual classroom was set up within Duolingo Schools for each participating cohort of students and they were encouraged to use the app on a regular basis. The tutor tools allowed the monitoring of how many days learners were active, how many lessons they completed, how many courses they completed, and how many points they were awarded while using Duolingo. These statistics were compared with

---

1. Coventry University, Coventry, England; lsx133@coventry.ac.uk; https://orcid.org/0000-0002-2256-7046

2. Coventry University, Coventry, England; lsx091@coventry.ac.uk; https://orcid.org/0000-0002-2754-5460

How to cite this chapter: Brick, B., & Cervi-Wilson, T. (2019). Enhancing learners' professional competence via Duolingo classroom. In C. Goria, L. Guetta, N. Hughes, S. Reisenleutner & O. Speicher (Eds), *Professional competencies in language learning and teaching* (pp. 19-29). Research-publishing.net. https://doi.org/10.14705/rpnet.2019.34.911

Chapter 2

the overall formal assessment grades on modules and further data was collected at the end of the project from a representative sample of learners (182) and tutors (ten) to establish whether the software influenced module marks.

Keywords: Duolingo, software, language learning, IWLP, CEFR A1.

1. Introduction

Language learning is increasingly taking place in a variety of formal and informal settings where mobile technologies and gamification have become more integrated into the language learning process. The vast number of opportunities to practise language learning outside the classroom provides instructors with the challenge of directing students towards resources most effective for their needs. One of these resources is Duolingo, a free language platform available both on PC and mobile. The site purports to teach nearly 2,000 vocabulary items for each language it offers and that studying via the app students are able to reach a vocabulary level of B1 on the CEFR if they complete all the activities available.

Duolingo delivers its content via a series of translation exercises, multiple choice quizzes, flashcards, word-pairing, and translating unknown words through clicking on them. In 2015, Duolingo Schools was launched which allows tutors to create virtual classrooms where they can assign specific homework tasks and challenges to students and monitor their progress. Alternatively, students can be challenged to study whatever they want on the platform in order to accumulate a target number of Duolingo Experience (XP) points which are awarded for successfully completing tasks on the site.

The self-directed learning skills students need to succeed on Duolingo help to develop professional competences essential for success on the job market such as autonomy, responsibility, motivation, self-efficacy, management, reflection, and persistence.

To contextualise this study, it is essential to understand that all UK universities are measured on the first jobs that their students acquire after graduation and therefore the employability skills of the graduates have become one of the most fundamental priorities in higher education (Routes into Languages, 2019).

In response to this, Coventry University implemented several new strategies to emphasise and stress the importance of education for employability. One of these strategies involved incorporating the teaching of employability skills into IWLP (Cervi-Wilson & Brick, 2016). IWLPs typically cater for students who want to study a language alongside their main degree subject. Uniquely, Coventry University offers language modules to undergraduate students as part of a scheme called Add+Vantage.

Typically, there are 24 students in each class and each class lasts for one hour and 40 minutes in total. The classes run over 11 weeks during which two weeks are used for assessment, leaving only nine full weeks of teaching. Much of the first class is taken up explaining how the module and assessments are organised and explaining to learners the procedures they are obliged to adhere to. This reduces the amount of contact time even further. As a result of this, students are encouraged to deepen their learning by practising what they have learnt in the classroom using a variety of self-directed learning tools such as Duolingo. Analysing students' use of language learning apps is extremely beneficial for instructors to understand where and how students focus their efforts outside the classroom. This study aims to establish whether or not widespread use of Duolingo has an impact on students' in class test performance in their language learning modules.

There have been numerous studies about Duolingo (Botero, Questier, & Zhu, 2018; García, 2013; Hermoso-Gómez, 2016; Krashen, 2014; Rosell-Aguilar, 2017; Teske, 2017; to name but a few) all of which have been critical of the product in numerous ways due to its repetitive nature, behaviouristic approach, the audiolingual method it adheres to in part, and the lack of opportunity for speaking practice. Its use of unauthentic voices for listening practice has also been widely criticised (Teske, 2017).

Chapter 2

Recent studies in Mobile Assisted Language Learning (MALL) literature (Chwo, Marek, & Wu, 2018) have revealed three common weaknesses. One is the discrepancy between how instructors think students use their devices and how they actually use them. The second relates to issues including motivation. This generally relates to the perceptions of students

> "concerning the usefulness of the MALL technology and lessons, and their resulting level of engagement in the MALL assignments, lessons, or activities. The third surrounds the short duration of MALL studies and poor research design" (Chwo et al., 2018, p. 62).

This study allowed students complete freedom to use the platform for self-directed learning and students were motivated, to some extent, by the link to achieving success on their IWLP module. What the study could not address was the duration of time students engaged in with the platform due to the fact that their IWLP course only lasted 11 weeks. In terms of research design, both quantitative and qualitative data were collected in order to triangulate results.

2. Methodology

The participants were IWLP students at Coventry University registered on degree courses across all disciplines and they are all expected to spend approximately ten hours per week on self-directed study. Students were introduced to the different features Duolingo offers and were asked to make an informed decision whether they wanted to be part of the project. Students were expected to monitor their own activity and interference by staff was kept to a minimum. There was no control group involved in this study due to ethical issues.

All staff teaching on European language Add+Vantage modules were invited to a meeting where the project was outlined to them and the process of setting up a classroom in Duolingo Schools, a separate platform which allows tutors to set homework and monitor student progress, was explained. Ethics forms were also distributed, but out of 35 members of staff teaching on the Add+Vantage language provision only 11 tutors were recruited, representing 182 students studying French, German, Spanish, and Italian at CEFR A1 level (see Figure 1 for breakdown).

Figure 1. Project participant language breakdown

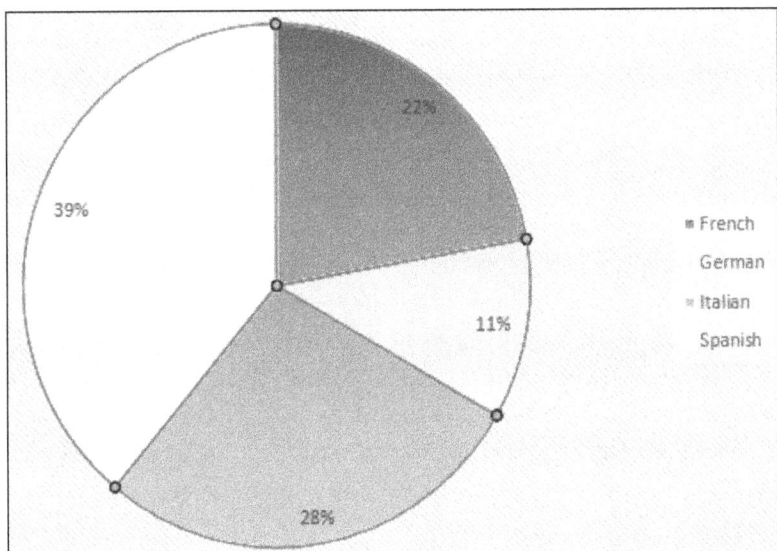

Some staff were already using Duolingo Schools, while others were interested in implementing it in their teaching. Anecdotal evidence suggested that students who regularly used Duolingo to practise what they had learnt in class achieved higher scores than those who had not engaged with the app. Therefore, the project sought to establish whether there was in fact a correlation between extensive use of Duolingo and achieving higher grades on the two courseworks that all Add+Vantage students are required to take. The data was collected for a period of 11 weeks which is the same period of time they spent studying on the Add+vantage programme. The tutor tools within Duolingo provided the necessary data to map against student performance. The data was generated in the form of XP points which students earned when they successfully completed tasks on the platform (Munday, 2016; Teske, 2017). In addition to this, each

Chapter 2

individual tutor set up small focus groups with their students to gather data regarding their experience of being involved in the project.

3. Results

At the end of the project, two sets of data were generated. The first one represented the marks that students had achieved by completing the required formal assessment for their module. The second set of data was generated by the Duolingo Schools platform and provided the exact number of XP points each participant had gathered during the project. The data was then merged to provide a graph correlating XP points against the overall coursework mark achieved by each participant. Details of these are provided in Figure 2, Figure 3, and Figure 4. The data was divided into three sections based on the number of XP points collected. Figure 2 shows the number of students who achieved up to 500 XP points, Figure 3 shows 500-1,000 and Figure 4 shows 1,000+. The quantitative results reveal some correlation between the number of XP points accumulated on Duolingo and the overall coursework mark achieved on the module.

Figure 2 shows that the vast majority of participants achieved fewer than 500 XP points throughout the duration of the project. The graph does not reveal a strong correlation between using Duolingo and performing well on the courseworks. In fact, 15% of participants achieved a mark above 80% and 4% failed the module.

Figure 3 shows that 13% of participants achieved between 500 and 1,000 XP points and of those 33% achieved a score above 80% on their coursework and all participants passed the module. However, 61% of this group scored between 40% and 60% on their coursework and only one failure was recorded.

The sample in Figure 4 is numerically far smaller than the other two groups but shows that 43% of participants who accumulated over 1,000 XP points achieved a module mark of over 80%. However, 21% of this group achieved a module mark ranging from 40% to 60% and one failure was recorded.

Figure 2. Participants scoring less than 500 XP points

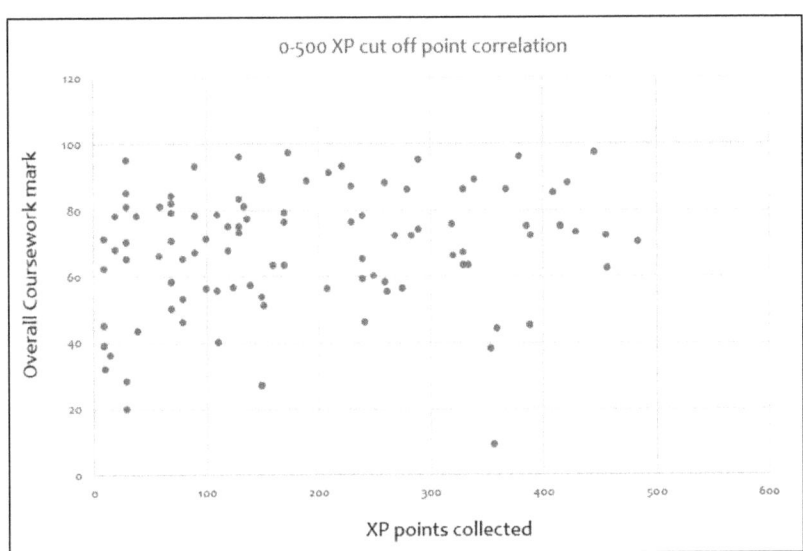

Figure 3. Participants scoring between 500 and 999 XP points

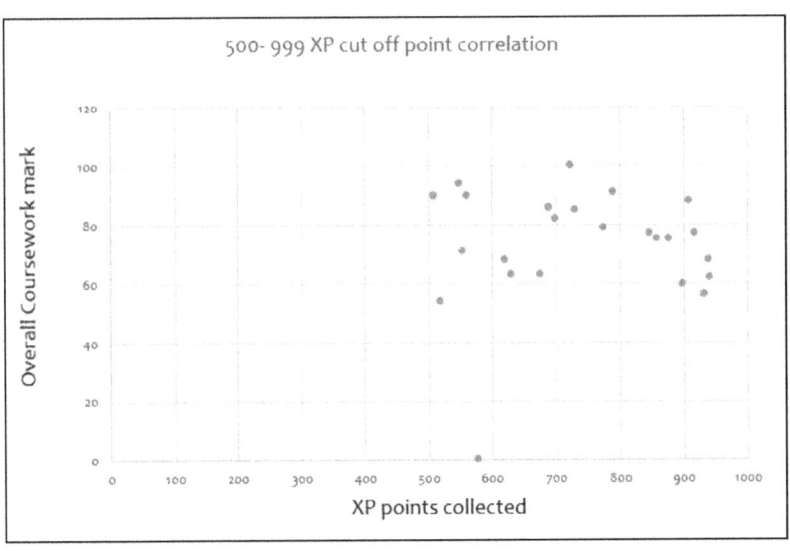

Chapter 2

Figure 4. Participants scoring more than 999 XP points

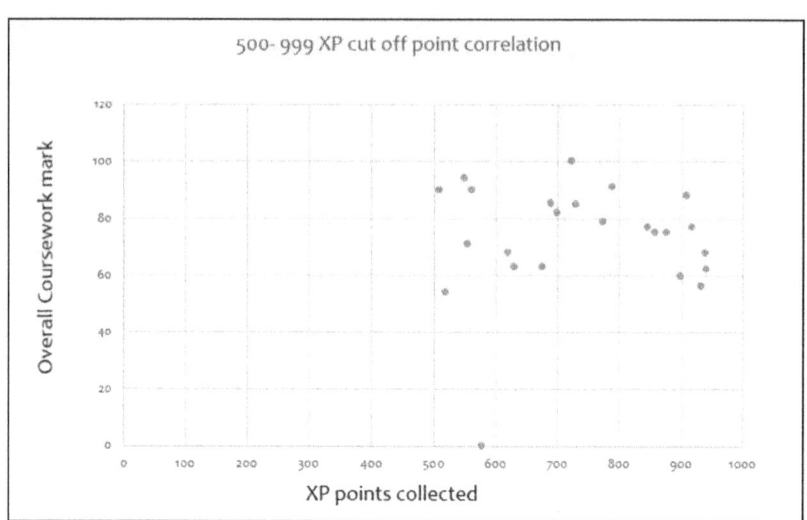

Overall the statistics show a slight correlation between the accumulation of XP points on Duolingo and achieving over 80% in the module courseworks.

The illustrative qualitative data revealed some further trends. Three of the participants were negative about Duolingo, describing it as boring and repetitive and criticising the lack of authentic audio available in the app. However, most of the responses collected from the focus group sessions revealed a positive experience using Duolingo, praising numerous features including the email reminders, the regular testing, the variety of activities and, in particular, how effective they found it when used in conjunction with formal learning undertaken in a classroom setting.

The following statements are representative of the comments collected from students by the tutors and form the qualitative results of the research:

> "Not many speaking activities and the voices aren't authentic" (Student A).

"It's boring at times and a bit repetitive" (Student B).

"I had tried to use it to learn another language without any assistance, but I did not find it quite as useful then" (Student C).

"Duolingo sends regular reminders" (Student D).

"It's a good opportunity to revise before a test" (Student E).

"There is so much variety. It gives us additional skills and experience" (Student F).

"In my experience Duolingo was quite useful, but more so when it was used in conjunction with a class or with some prior knowledge of the language" (Student G).

"When I used it for Italian, in combination with what I'd learned in class, I thought it was quite effective because it used active recall revision tactics, which I know help me learn best" (Student H).

"The fact that the things I had got wrong were tested again at the end of each 'session'" (Student I).

"It was also very helpful to see where my strengths and weaknesses were with learning Italian" (Student J).

"Overall, I thought Duolingo was a useful tool for me in studying Italian. I don't know if it helped me to improve my grade because I used it in combination with other tools, such as languagesonline, my notes from the class and the textbook. Some 'sessions' in Duolingo were obviously more relevant to the class content than others, so I don't know if there was a correlation between my Duolingo use and my marks" (Student K).

4. Conclusions

The quantitative data revealed a slight correlation between obtaining over 100 Duolingo XP points over an 11-week period and achieving an above average mark in the module assessment. The qualitative data revealed differing attitudes amongst participants, but the majority were overall positive about the app when they used the tool in conjunction with regular attendance at a language learning class.

The study itself has its limitations partly due to the relatively small sample and the duration, common to many MALL studies as mentioned above (Chwo et al., 2018). Even though 456 students were approached to take part in the project, only 182 (40%) agreed to share their data with us. It was also impossible to isolate Duolingo as the only source of extra-curricular study. The data collected was only based on the accumulation of XP points, which only provided an overview of the amount of activities participants undertook, rather than a more focussed approach on specific tasks assigned by the tutor within the app itself. It was also apparent that some tutors encouraged the students to use the app on a regular basis more than others.

Finally, we can conclude that Duolingo may be used most effectively as a supplementary language learning tool to consolidate and deepen knowledge acquired in a classroom setting rather than as a sole source.

References

Botero, G., Questier, F., Zhu, C. (2018). Self-directed language learning in a mobile-assisted, out-of-class context: do students walk the walk the talk? *Computer Assisted Language Learning*, early view. https://doi.org/10.1080/09588221.2018.1485707

Cervi-Wilson, T., & Brick, B. (2016). The employability advantage: embedding skills through a university-wide language programme. In E. Corradini, K. Borthwick & A. Gallagher-Brett (Eds), *Employability for languages: a handbook* (pp. 149-153). Research-publishing.net. https://doi.org/10.14705/rpnet.2016.cbg2016.476

Chwo, G. S. M., Marek, M. W., & Wu, W.-C. V. (2018). Meta-analysis of MALL research and design. *System, 74*, 62-72. https://doi.org/10.1016/j.system.2018.02.009

García, I. (2013). Learning a language for free while translating the web. Does Duolingo work? *International Journal of English Linguistics, 3*(1), 19-25. https://doi.org/10.5539/ijel.v3n1p19

Hermoso-Gómez, B. (2016). Duolingo, an app for learning languages, *The Language Scholar*, University of Leeds.

Krashen, S. (2014). Does Duolingo "trump" university-level language learning? *International Journal of Foreign Language Teaching, 9*(1), 13-15.

Munday, P. (2016). The case for using DUOLINGO as part of the language classroom experience. *Revista Iberoamericana de Educación a Distancia, 19*(1), 83-101.

Rosell-Aguilar, F. (2017). State of the app: a taxonomy and framework for evaluating language learning mobile applications. *Calico, 34*(2), 243-258.

Routes into Languages. (2019). *Employability*. https://www.routesintolanguages.ac.uk/resources/employability

Teske, K. (2017). Duolingo. *Calico Learning Technology Review, 34*(3), 393-401.

3 Enhancing independent learning competence and grammar language learning strategies

Jumana Ghannam[1]

Abstract

In an ever-evolving competitive world, learning a Foreign Language (FL) has become essential. To enhance learners' learning proficiency, learners should be encouraged to build the necessary competence for learning an FL, and this could be done by enhancing the employment of Language Learning Strategies (LLSs), as LLSs constitute an essential aspect of boosting and promoting the learning process (Chamot, 2001; Griffiths, 2003; Griffiths & Oxford, 2014; Oxford, 1990; Rubin, 1975). They have a persuasive and advocate role as an aid for learners to boost and improve their language learning proficiency, and have been explored by researchers since the 1970's. Despite the crucial developments on LLSs since the 1970's, Grammar Learning Strategies (GLSs) are in their infant stage in the field. LLSs researchers have not given as much attention to GLSs as to the other language skills; therefore, GLSs have largely been ignored (Anderson, 2005; Cohen, 2011; Cohen, Pinilla-Herrera, Thompson, & Witzig, 2001; Oxford, Lee, & Park, 2007; Pawlak, 2009a; Pawlak, 2012). For example, Oxford et al. (2007, p. 117) called GLSs the "Second Cinderella" of LLSs research. This paper will report a study that aimed at enhancing independent learning competence through employing GLSs by investigating how FL learners develop their GLSs and how they solve their grammar learning problems using such strategies. Research participants were male and female university students studying different European and non-European languages.

---

1. Nottingham Trent University, Nottingham, England; jumana.ghannam@ntu.ac.uk

How to cite this chapter: Ghannam, J. (2019). Enhancing independent learning competence and grammar language learning strategies. In C. Goria, L. Guetta, N. Hughes, S. Reisenleutner & O. Speicher (Eds), *Professional competencies in language learning and teaching* (pp. 31-40). Research-publishing.net. https://doi.org/10.14705/rpnet.2019.34.912

Chapter 3

>The results show the high rate of using cognitive GLSs especially in explicit inductive and explicit deductive learning to promote their independent language learning competence to face their grammar learning difficulties.
>
>**Keywords: grammar learning strategies, promoting learning proficiency, independent language learning competence.**

1. Introduction

Since the seventies, there has been a great recognition that LLSs are "an extremely powerful learning tool" (O'Malley et al., 1985, p. 43). LLSs enhance learners' learning proficiency and help to build the necessary independent learning competence as they constitute an essential aspect of enhancing and promoting the learning process (Chamot, 2001; Griffiths, 2003; Griffiths & Oxford, 2014; Oxford, 1990; Rubin, 1975). Despite of all the useful work in the LLSs field, GLSs are in their developing stage. The aim of this study is to contribute to the literature and to enhance independent learning competence through GLSs by investigating how FL learners develop their GLSs and how they solve their grammar learning problems using such strategies.

2. Literature review

Literature ascertains that LLSs offer benefits to learners, especially the benefits of making learning an FL easy, proficient, and effective. Rubin (1975) defines LLSs as "techniques or devices which a learner may use to acquire knowledge" (p. 43). Skehan (1989) views them as "an explosion of activity" (p. 285). O'Malley et al. (1985) define them as "an extremely powerful learning tool" (p. 43). Oxford (1990) defines LLSs as "specific actions and steps taken by the learner to make learning easier, faster, more enjoyable, more self-directed, more effective, and more transferable to new situations" (p. 8). Griffiths (2008) proposes an operational definition of LLSs as "[a]ctivities consciously chosen by learners for the purpose of regulating their own language learning" (p. 87). Oxford's (2017) definition summarises all previous definitions. She defines LLSs as complex dynamic thoughts and actions selected and used by learners with some degree of consciousness in specific contexts in order to regulate multiple aspects of themselves to (1) accomplish language tasks, (2) enhance language performance, and use, and/or (3) improve long-term proficiency. Learners often use strategies flexibly and creatively to meet their learning needs.

Nevertheless, grammar plays a very important role in language learning, like the other aspects of the language, as learning grammar efficiently equips learners with a basis which aids them to construct their knowledge and empowers them to use the FL effectively (Ellis, 2006). Learners use certain strategies when learning grammar to enhance their grammar learning proficiency and to make language learning and language use easier, more effective, and more efficient as these strategies control and facilitate the learning process (Griffiths, 2008; Oxford et al., 2007).

In order to fill the existing gap in GLSs, this study investigated how FL learners solve their language grammar learning problems using GLSs and how they have developed them. Oxford et al. (2007) proposed a GLSs taxonomy by distinguishing three categories. They allied the categories into the grammar teaching instructions: first, GLSs are reflective of implicit language learning that focusses on form; second, GLSs based on explicit inductive language learning when learners participate in rule-discovery; and third, GLSs applicable to explicit deductive learning and learners apply the rules in different activities. However, this classification was criticised; for instance, Pawlak (2009b) argues that Oxford et al.'s (2007) classification links grammar learning strategies to grammar teaching methods and it neglects the existing LLSs classifications: cognitive, memory, compensation, metacognitive, affective, and social strategies (see Table 1). Pawlak (2013) offered a GLSs classification which combines LLSs classification in addition to grammar learning methods. Therefore, this study will employ Pawlak's (2013) classification (see Table 2) to analyse the data.

Table 1. Oxford's (1990, p. 17) taxonomy of LLSs

Direct Strategies	Memory Strategies	Creating mental links
		Applying images and sounds
		Reviewing well
		Employing action
	Cognitive Strategies	Practising
		Receiving and sending messages strategies
		Analysing and reasoning
		Creating structure for input and output
	Compensation Strategies	Guessing intelligently
		Overcoming limitations in speaking and writing
Indirect Strategies	Metacognitive Strategies	Creating your learning
		Arranging and planning your learning
		Evaluating your learning
	Affective Strategies	Lowering your anxiety
		Encouraging yourself
		Taking your emotional temperature
	Social Strategies	Asking questions
		Cooperating with others
		Empathising with others

Table 2. Based on Pawlak's (2013) classification

Cognitive Strategies	GLSs for the grammar in communication
	GLSs for developing explicit knowledge of grammar: • GLSs used for deductive learning • GLSs used for inductive learning
	GLSs employed to develop implicit knowledge of grammar: • GLSs for comprehending grammar and understanding form-meaning • GLSs for producing grammar in controlled and in communicative practice
	GLSs employed to deal with corrective feedback on grammar errors in a produced piece of work
Metacognitive Strategies	Manage and supervise the process of FL learning grammar through the procedures of organising, planning, monitoring, and evaluating

Affective Strategies	Self-regulating motivations and emotions when learning grammar
Social Strategies	Interaction with the FL proficient users or other peers to enhance the process of grammar learning

3. Methodology

Since this study focusses on the process of developing GLSs and on how learners overcome learning grammar problems they might face when learning grammar of an FL, qualitative methods were used. Therefore, semi structured interviews were conducted on 34 participants. Interviews gave a degree of freedom to obtain deep data and ask more questions (Bryman, 2012; Cohen, Manion, & Morrison, 2011; Rubin & Rubin, 2005). The questions were designed in a way that helped interviewees think about how they develop their GLSs and how they solve their grammar learning problems using these strategies. The general questions used to investigate how learners solve their language grammar learning problems and how they have developed their GLSs were: (1) 'What are the problems you face when learning grammar?', (2) 'How do you overcome these problems?', and (3) 'How did you come to use these GLSs?'. In some situations, the interview questions were followed up with some additional inquiries to prod the participants to provide more details. Interviews were audio-recorded and the recordings were transcribed and subjected to qualitative analysis. Data obtained from the interview was rich and varied.

3.1. Participants

Research participants were male and female university students studying different European and non-European languages. Their age ranged from 21 to 50 and their proficiency level varied from beginners to intermediate level. They come from a variety of educational backgrounds. They attend two hours per week of class contact time over one full academic year. The aim of the research was communicated with them, which resulted in their enthusiastic voluntary participation in the interviews. They signed a consent form.

3.2. Data analysis

The interviews were analysed using thematic analysis recommended by Braun and Clarke (2006). All GLSs that the informants referred to were identified, coded and categorised. The process was completed in several iterations. The categorisation highlighted similarities in the participants' responses. The responses were categorised according to number of themes to help adding all the responses, even the unexpected ones. Links between the research questions and the themes were carefully and thoroughly examined.

4. Results and discussion

Learners' development of cognitive, metacognitive, affective, and social strategies varies. It was surprising to find that most of the participants exhibited resourceful knowledge about GLSs and how they were developed and used effectively to face learning grammar problems. The findings of the study showed that most GLSs categories were developed and used by all participants. The results also confirmed that there was a high use of GLSs especially among those language learners who have been learning more than one FL. Certain GLSs were consistently considered to have a substantial effect on overcoming learning grammar problems that learners face. For instance, most participants agreed on the effectiveness of the cognitive strategies, especially in explicit learning which was detected in the case of "revising regularly", "practising over and over", and "memorizing rules". They predominantly mentioned engaging in practice to understand and control sentence structure by 'doing exercises' that have highly controlled activities, such as multiple choice and/or gap filling. On the other hand, the affective strategies were deemed not significant by most participants. Social strategies were given much less importance overall as there was little evidence for their application in the interviews.

In terms of developing their GLSs, it was found that with time, learners developed their GLSs and became familiar with the intricacies of developing their own GLSs. They appreciated the significance and effectiveness of GLSs in facing their learning grammar of the FL and making learning more effective and enjoyable. Some reported that they came to know some GLSs from past tutors and fellow students. However, over the years, they adopted their own strategies from a variety of different sources, such as other language learners, websites, and books. However, most participants developed their GLSs through 'self-discovery' and 'trial and error'. They tried numerous techniques until they found the most effective and convenient ones when they faced a new grammar point. Some participants adopted these helpful and convenient strategies and adapted them according to the situation. They mentioned that they tried to investigate more about the techniques by employing them in different situations, while others used different steps and techniques each time according to the situation. They mentioned that they found that these techniques support their grammar learning and use in different situations; therefore, they were adopted. Participants found that the development of the GLSs went through modification stages according to the situation and the nature of the grammar item.

Based on these findings, an effort is made to offer answers to this study's questions. Regarding the use of all GLSs, there are bases for optimism as learners are aware of GLSs and aware of their effectiveness in solving grammar-learning problems. One possible interpretation is that since the process of FL learning is a complex process, it needs various learning strategies, and literature shows that most language learners use learning strategies to aid their learning (O'Malley & Chamot, 1990; Oxford, 1990; Oxford et al., 2007). Therefore, it is logical to find that learners in this study use GLSs as these GLSs support overcoming impediments.

With respect to the predominant use of cognitive strategies, this might be due to the type of the grammar tasks which require practice, and it might be because learners have their preferred method of facing grammar problems which is more convenient to their cognitive experiences and styles. Another reason might be due to participants' FL proficiency level, as less proficient learners use more cognitive strategies and are mainly keen to seek practice opportunities. This is in line with O'Malley et al.'s (1985) study, as they found that beginner level Russian and Spanish English as a FL learners use cognitive strategies the most and more than the intermediate level learners. In addition, this is in line with the findings of Pawlak (2012), as in his study he found that about 74% of students refer to the use of 'doing exercises' for learning grammar.

Concerning the social strategies, a potential explanation for reporting social strategies as less important is that FL learners prefer to learn grammar explicitly rather than implicitly, as practising with native speakers might not give them the opportunity to learn grammar rules explicitly. This finding is consistent with that of second language acquisition researchers, such as DeKeyser (2003). They believe that cognitive and linguistic developmental stages of the adult FL learners need explicit learning; therefore, their GLSs are concerned with paying attention to forms and grammar rules as this aids learners edit their errors. Another possible explanation for social strategies to be less used is that explicit information contributes to the improvement of implicit knowledge, and after mastering the grammar item, they feel more comfortable and confident making friends with native speakers to practise what they have learnt. Ellis (2006) observes that explicit knowledge could contribute to the improvement and development of implicit knowledge when learners can process input and intake.

5. Conclusion

When combining the findings, I come to the conclusions that learners employ various GLSs to promote their independent language learning competence to overcome their grammar learning difficulties and to enhance their grammar learning proficiency. Cogitative strategies were the most used strategies among less proficient FL learners. Social strategies were given much less importance by the participants. However, affective strategies were deemed not significant. The findings of this study were in line with some relevant studies. In terms of developing GLSs, most GLSs were developed by trial and error and self-discovery.

Acknowledgements

The work has been supported by Dr Gloria Gutierrez.

References

Anderson, N. (2005). L2 learning strategies. In E. Hinkel (Ed.), *Handbook of research in second language teaching and learning* (pp. 757-772). Lawrence Erlbaum Associates.

Braun, V., & Clarke, V. (2006). Using thematic analysis in psychology. *Qualitative Research in Psychology, 3*(2), 77-101. https://doi.org/10.1191/1478088706qp063oa

Bryman, A. (2012). *Social research methods* (4th ed.). Oxford University Press.

Chamot, A. U. (2001). The role of learning strategies in second language acquisition. In M. P. Breen (Ed.), *Learner contributions to language learning new direction in research* (pp. 25-43). Pearson Education Limited.

Cohen, A. D. (2011). *Strategies in learning and using a second language*. Routledge.

Cohen, A. D., Pinilla-Herrera, A., Thompson, J. R., & Witzig, L. E. (2001). Communicating grammatically: evaluating a learner strategy website for Spanish grammar. *CALICO Journal, 29*(1), 145-172. https://doi.org/10.11139/cj.29.1.145-172

Cohen, L., Manion, L., & Morrison, K. (2011). *Research methods in education* (7th ed.). Routledge.

DeKeyser, R. (2003). Implicit and explicit learning. In C. J. Doughty & M. H. Long (Eds), *The handbook of second language acquisition* (pp. 313-348). Blackwell Publishing.

Ellis, R. (2006). Current issues in the teaching of grammar: an SLA perspective. *TESOL Quarterly 40*(1), 83-107. https://doi.org/10.2307/40264512

Griffiths, C. (2003). Patterns of language learning strategies use. *System, 31*, 367-383.

Griffiths, C. (2008). Strategies and good language learners. In Griffiths, C. (Ed.), *Lessons form good language learners* (pp. 83-98). Cambridge University Press. https://doi.org/10.1017/cbo9780511497667.009

Griffiths, C., & Oxford, R. L. (2014). The twenty-first century landscape of language learning strategies: introduction to this special issue. *System, 43*, 1-10. https://doi.org/10.1016/j.system.2013.12.009

O'Malley, J. M., & Chamot, A. (1990). *Learning strategies in second language acquisition*. Cambridge University Press.

O'Malley, J. M., Chamot, A., Stewner-Manzanares, G., Küpper, L., & Russo, P. R. (1985). Learning strategies used by beginning and intermediate ESL students. *Language Learning, 35*(1), 21-46.

Oxford, R. L. (1990). *Language learning strategies: what every teacher should know*. Heinle and Heinle.

Oxford, R. L. (2017). *Teaching and researching language learning strategies. Self-regulation in context*. Routledge.

Oxford. R. L., Lee, K., & Park, G. (2007). L2 grammar strategies: the second Cinderella and beyond. In A. D. Cohen & E. Macaro (Eds), *Language learner strategies* (pp. 117-139). Oxford University Press.

Pawlak, M. (2009a). Grammar learning strategies and language attainment: seeking a relationship. *Research in Language, 7*(1), 43-60. https://doi.org/10.2478/v10015-009-0004-7

Pawlak, M. (2009b). *Investigating grammar-learning strategies: in search of appropriate research tools*. Paper presented at the 19th Conference of the European Second Language Association, Cork, 2-5 September.

Pawlak, M. (2012). Instructional mode and the use of grammar learning strategies. In M. Pawlak (Ed.), *New perspectives on individual differences in language learning and teaching* (pp. 263-287). Springer. https://doi.org/10.1007/978-3-642-20850-8_17

Pawlak, M. (2013). Researching grammar learning strategies: combining the macro- and micro perspective. In Ł. Salski, W. Szubko-Sitarek & J. Majer (Eds), *Perspectives on foreign language learning* (pp. 191-220). University of Łódź Press.

Rubin, H. J., & Rubin, I. (2005). *Qualitative interviewing: the art of hearing data* (2nd ed.). Sage. https://doi.org/10.4135/9781452226651

Rubin, J. (1975). What the "good language learner" can teach us. *TESOL Quarterly, 9*(1), 41-51. https://doi.org/10.2307/3586011

Skehan, P. (1989). *Individual differences in second-language learning*. Edward Arnold.

4. Training language professionals to be digitally proficient in an undergraduate and postgraduate context

María Jordano de la Torre[1]

Abstract

The last five years have been witnessing the publication of two crucial documents in the field of language teaching and technology: 'CEFR: Companion Volume with New Descriptors' (Council of Europe, 2018) and 'DigCompEdu' (Punie & Redecker, 2017). These publications will be decisive for the design of new study plans aimed at the training of language teachers at all levels. This article describes the connection found between the second mentioned document and two of the subjects delivered by the researcher. One of these subjects is offered optionally in the fourth course of the bachelor's degree in English studies, and the other one is included within the second year of a master on Information and Communication Technology (ICT) applied to language studies. Since the launch of both subjects in 2009 and 2010 respectively, the enrolled students have been providing detailed feedback about their digital competence levels and the course itself. These data, added to the information retrieved from the satisfaction questionnaires distributed by our university, have contributed to depict a detailed map of the level of digital competences of students who come from different parts of Spain and other countries.

Keywords: digital competences, teacher training, distance education, collaborative learning.

---

1. Universidad Nacional de Educación a Distancia (UNED), Madrid, Spain; mjordano@flog.uned.es; http://orcid.org/0000-0001-7779-9584

How to cite this chapter: Jordano de la Torre, M. (2019). Training language professionals to be digitally proficient in an undergraduate and postgraduate context. In C. Goria, L. Guetta, N. Hughes, S. Reisenleutner & O. Speicher (Eds), *Professional competencies in language learning and teaching* (pp. 41-52). Research-publishing.net. https://doi.org/10.14705/rpnet.2019.34.913

Chapter 4

1. Introduction

Being digitally competent was a skill perceived as an added value when referring to teaching some years ago. Nowadays, a minimum of technical training is required for most teachers at all stages across different disciplines. For this reason, several American and European organisations are interested in promoting competence-based training all around the world. Some authors in favour of these initiatives conceive digital literacy skills as a development that "should be an integral part of pre- and in-service training programs" (Hauck & Kurek, 2017, p. 2). The Qingdao Declaration includes an item with the same idea: "11. Successful integration of ICT into teaching and learning requires rethinking the role of teachers and reforming their preparation and professional development" (UNESCO, 2015, p. 5).

This chapter studies the evolution of the digital competences level of the students of two subjects offered by the Faculty of Philology of the Universidad Nacional de Educación a Distancia (UNED), the Spanish Open University since the first years of delivery. The singularity of this study remains on the heterogeneity of its participants, since they come from different parts of the state (including other nationalities), share varied academic interests (e.g. translation, language teaching, or the publishing industry among others), and begin their studies from a diverse digital background. Thanks to the continuous adaptation to the digital competences frameworks published by international institutions and the yearly feedback collected from the students, these subjects have achieved their actual appearance. This work explains some of the most relevant actions carried out to adapt them to contemporary times.

2. Training language professionals through competences

Language teachers have been pioneers in the use of technology in the classroom. They have seen the Internet as an unlimited source of authentic texts to exploit actively or as a place to promote communication among different language speakers. Today, having the Internet as a resource or space to exchange is not enough. We are living in the era of social networks and apps for everything, so our students demand learning methods adapted to those needs.

Broadly speaking, it can be stated that the first step given for deciding which digital competences were relevant for teaching was the elaboration of a report named 'ICT Competency Standards for Teachers: Policy Framework' (UNESCO, 2008). The main aims of this work were: to serve as a guideline for the professional development providers, to unify the vocabulary related to the ICT in learning environments, and proposing the necessary digital competences common to all teachers. These competences would need to be acquired at different approaches/stages: technology literacy, knowledge deepening, and knowledge creation (UNESCO, 2008, p. 8). Three years later, the same institution proposed a second version of the aforementioned report in collaboration with Microsoft. The authors highlighted the importance of being able to train teachers to be digitally competent so that they could later teach their students with the most appropriate ICT tools (UNESCO, 2011, p. 3). The three stages proposed by the UNESCO might be referred to seven different elements (see Table 1).

Table 1. The UNESCO ICT competency framework for teachers (UNESCO, 2011, p. 3)

	Technology Literacy	Knowledge Deepening	Knowledge Creation
Understanding ICT in education	Policy awareness	Policy understanding	Policy innovation
Curriculum and assessment	Basic knowledge	Knowledge application	Knowledge society skills
Pedagogy	Integrate technology	Complex problem solving	Self-management
ICT	Basic tools	Complex tools	Pervasive tools
Organisation and administration	Standard classroom	Collaborative groups	Learning organisations
Teacher professional learning	Digital literacy	Manage and guide	Teacher as model learner

As can be perceived from the information contained in the table above, the level of autonomy and complexity increases from left to right. This progressive increase of difficulty will help the different models of Information Technology (IT) certification to delimit and describe the contents of each stage. The improvements of this updating add a more detailed explanation of each competency per stage/level of proficiency, which is also accompanied by some specific examples.

It was 2013 when, retaking the recommendations given by the European Parliament (2006), the European Commission elaborated another report to expand on one of the eight competences included, digital competence (listed in the fourth place). It was described as the competence which

> "involves the confident and critical use of Information Society Technology (IST) for work, leisure and communication. It is underpinned by basic skills in ICT: the use of computers to retrieve, assess, store, produce, present and exchange information, and to communicate and participate in collaborative networks via the Internet" (European Parliament, 2006, p. 15).

These five actions proposed for the citizens to be digitally competent were identified as the five main areas of the DIGComp 1.0: information, communication, content creation, safety, and problem solving. Each of these competence areas was divided into different dimensions, and, at the same time, these dimensions split into levels of complexity (Ferrari, 2013). These levels (A-Foundation, B-Intermediate, C-Advanced) correspond to the three stages proposed by UNESCO (2011).

Two years later, ministers of education, teachers' organisations, personnel from different educational stages and members of the private sectors, among others, agreed on the Qingdao Declaration to "reduce the long-existing learning divide" (UNESCO, 2015, p. 3). This is one of the reasons why they concentrated on the less favoured layers of society by encouraging the promotion of open educational resources such as massive open online courses or open libraries.

The first updating of the DIGComp 2.0 document appeared in 2016 as "the key set of competences needed for personal development, social inclusion, active citizenship and employment" (Vuorikari, Punie, Carretero, & Van Den Brande, 2016, p. 2). One of the major changes consists of the updating of the five competence areas as shown in Table 2. Two years later, the update Phase 2.1 was published, which was featured by adding eight proficiency levels to the DigComp 2.1., as an evolution of the three stages proposed by UNESCO. This improvement is due to the division of the previous levels into two and adding a new double level to these three, named 'high-specialised'.

Table 2. Areas of digital competence based on DigComp 1.0 (Vuorikari et al., 2016, p. 12)

	Competence areas version 1.0	Competence areas version 2.0
Inter-related areas with overlapping	1. Information	1. Information and data literacy
	2. Communication	2. Communication and collaboration
	3. Content creation	3. Digital Content creation
Cross-cutting across	4. Safety	4. Safety
	5. Problem-solving	5. Problem-solving

Based on the digital skills competences previously described, different public and private institutions began to design several placement tests to measure the IT level of the citizens and employees with the aim of certifying their digital competence. Some of these diagnostic tools are the International Computer Driving Licence (ICDL), Ikanos[2] (Pais Vasco), ACTIC (Catalonia), or the diagnosis platform created by Andalusia[3].

Almost parallel to the launching of the second revision of the DigComp, a new framework specialised in education was published: DigCompEDU (Punie & Redecker, 2017). This document proposes a new nomenclature for the DigComp descriptors so that they can be more related to activities contextualised in different learning environments, along with its descriptors: A1 (Newcomer), A2

---

2. http://test.ikanos.eus/index.php/566697?lang=en

3. http://www.digcomp.andaluciaesdigital.es/

(Explorer), B1 (Integrator), B2 (Expert), C1 (Leader), C2 (Pioneer). Similarly to what happened to the already mentioned tools designed to calibrate the digital proficiency of the citizens, other platforms like the Digital Competence Portfolio for Teachers have also been created by other institutions, like the Spanish Ministry of Education[4] in 2017.

In the case of language teachers, two placement tests must be highlighted: eGRID[5] (final product of a European project to assess language teachers, teacher trainers, and managers) and The Digital Teacher (elaborated by the Cambridge Assessment English)[6]. Both consist of an online form which generates a final printable diagnosis with the IT level of the user. Although language learning is not the main focus of the subjects dealt with in this study, both tests are being evaluated and tested every year by the group of students with closer interests towards language teaching.

3. Methodology

Part of the aims of this work consist in explaining the treatment of digital competences by different international institutions to justify the contents included in the selected subjects. After having considered the different initiatives described, this study proposes an approach to include specific activities in the curriculum to work on the DigComp descriptors. All the activities worked with undergraduate and graduate students are being updated yearly to their own needs as required by the action research methodology followed (Burns, 2010; Ivankova, 2014; Klein, 2012). The same four steps are given every year: planning, acting, observing, and reflecting (Putman & Rock, 2017), taking into account that the planning stage takes place even before the beginning of the academic year. Most of the improvements made in the new course come from the observation and reflecting stage from the previous

---

4. https://portfolio.intef.es/
5. http://egrid.epg-project.eu/en/egrid
6. https://thedigitalteacher.com/framework

year. Thanks to this process, the institutional satisfaction questionnaire results obtain better results every year.

3.1. ICT for English studies

This is an optional subject which is taught in the fourth course of the bachelor's degree in English studies. It is comprised of five European Credit Transfer and Accumulation System (ECTS) points, is delivered in the first semester, and has achieved a total of 230 students in the year 2017-2018. Its main goal is making the student competent in digital skills either in a short-term future (elaboration of their final degree project) or in a long-term future (e.g. their professional career). The publishing industry, language teaching, translation, researching, or archiving are among the professional outcomes preferred by these students once they finish. Consequently, the syllabus has been designed from a broad and flexible perspective, taking into consideration an assortment of scenarios. Among the software selected to pursue this aim, we highlight Mendeley, used to build and manage collaborative bibliographic references, GoConqr, an authoring tool to create online quizzes and interactive contents, and academic social networks, used to be able to spread their knowledge and learn directly from specialised authors. GoConqr was a tool proposed some years after the launching of this subject as a way to prepare the test exam that they had to pass at the end of the course. This action has brought successful results and it is the reason why we are still making use of it year after year, even recycling quizzes created by other students in the past[7]. It also served to develop the third DigComp competence, which is 'content creation'.

3.2. Teaching and processing foreign languages in collaborative work environments

It is a five ECTS point subject offered optionally by the master's degree in ICT in language education and processing (UNED). It receives approximately 20 students per year, most of them being graduates in education, language

---

7. https://www.goconqr.com/es-ES/groups/38516/show_study_aids

studies, translation, or even computer sciences. Apart from using Mendeley to share and manage bibliographical references, the students are encouraged to use collaborative tools to communicate and create wikis, or blogs. Once the students try one of the suggested tools, they are suggested to comment on their experiences on the forum so that they can enrich others with different perspectives. These resources are elaborated from scratch and focussed on new topics proposed by the teaching team every year. They would have to spread the resulting products through different social networks, including a later analysis of the generated statistics to be presented orally at the end of the course.

All the tools used have been accurately selected so that they learn how to use them later in their work as language teachers with their students or as members of institutions interested in working collaboratively in their everyday routine. All the activities generated will be transcribed in a final assignment, in a portfolio format, so that the tutors and teaching staff can evaluate it.

4. Results

Most of the students enrolled at distance universities like UNED share a common factor: extreme heterogeneity. Some of them already have higher studies in opposition to those who abandoned their compulsory studies very early, others are working in related or not so related fields to the degree they are studying, and others live far away from Spain. All these elements have pushed the researcher to elaborate a brief survey at the beginning of the course to obtain a general idea of the sort of needs required by the students of each academic year. The collected results show an increasing evolution towards a better knowledge of digital competences (e.g. social networks or mobile technology), although there are some gaps which remain almost identical (e.g. informational literacy).

Subjects like the ones described in this study have been specially designed to soften the deficiencies described in Figure 1 with the help of the contents shown in Table 3. Two years ago, the form from Figure 1 was substituted by a new one to know the level of expertise the specific tools dealt with in the course. Seventy-one percent of the respondents of the new form affirmed to know Google Drive in opposition to 4% who declared using Microsoft OneDrive. This fact has made the teaching team reinforce the number of activities related to the Office 365 tool, at the same time as bettering their own institutional applications.

Figure 1. Percentage of the students who do not know the selected ICT tools (2011-2017)

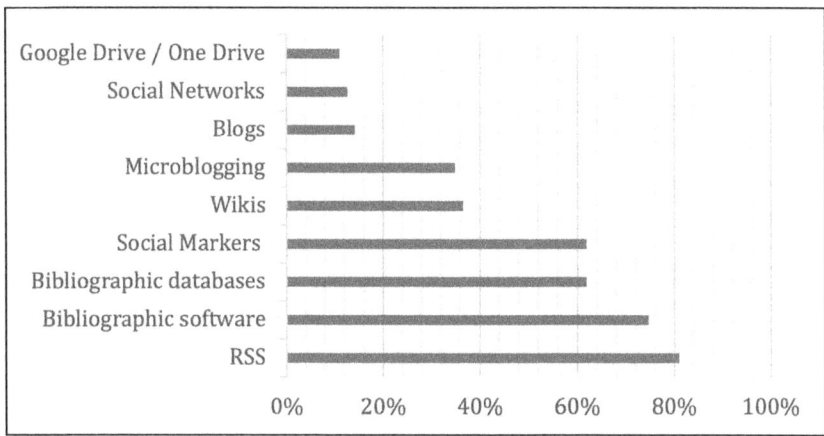

Although each course has its own syllabus, the methodology used in both subjects is very similar, except for activities which cannot be applied to numerous groups. Table 3 shows the contents of both courses and the relation of their contents to the competences of the DigComp. Hence, the information literacy (1) covers the first two units of the undergraduate course and only the first one in the postgrad subject; the communication competence (2) is covered by two units in the first subject and one in the second, although it is also worked transversally throughout the subject due to its collaborative nature; content creation (3) is deeply dealt with in the second and third units from the postgrad subject, apart from being more superficially covered by the last unit of the undergraduate subject with the content edition; and problem solving (4) has been worked transversally in the postgrad subject and more superficially in the fifth unit of the undergraduate subject, through the accessibility topics.

Chapter 4

Table 3. Course contents and their relation to DigComp contents

DigComp competences	APLICACIONES DE LAS TIC EN LOS ESTUDIOS INGLESES (4th grade – Bachelor's Degree)	DigComp competences	TEACHING AND PROCESSING FOREIGN LANGUAGES IN COLLABORATIVE WORK ENVIRONMENTS (Master, optional)
1 Information literacy	1. Information retrieval with ICT: English Studies Databases and Electronic Libraries	1 Information literacy	1. Working on the Internet
	2. Bibliographic management applications	3 Content creation	2. The use of wikis as a collaborative working space to deal with foreign languages
2 Communication	3. Communities of practice tools		3. The use of blogs in a foreign language teaching and learning context
	4. Web 2.0 and other emerging technologies applied to research	2 Communication	4. Social networks applied to foreign languages learning
3 Content creation/5 Problem solving	5. Software applications revision: research and the publishing industry	4 Safety	5. The use of web-based tools for monitoring and feedback retrieval in a foreign language context

As it can be observed, all the units included in both subjects cover most of the competences included in the DigComp documents, although they have been adapted to the needs of the different courses. The number of students has also conditioned the type of activity proposed, since 240 students cannot receive the same attention than the postgrad students (approximately 20 students per year).

5. Conclusion

We live in an era surrounded by technological applications which grow in number and complexity as times passes. The new generations require drastic changes in education and the way to prepare them for the professional future evolve as well. Our teaching methods cannot be based on a fixed methodology which teaches how to use specific software and finishes with its evaluation. We must use technological subjects like the ones described in this study to give a step forward, teaching students to walk alone in a never-ending process of lifelong learning. To achieve this, a continuous cycle of improvement based on the students' feedback is required so that our digital competence can grow at the same pace as technological advances, as the action research defends. Trying something new for the first time is time-consuming, but it is worth it to improve the quality of our teaching and keep it alive.

References

Burns, A. (2010). *Doing action research in English language teaching: a guide for practitioners*. Routledge.

Council of Europe. (2018). *Common European Framework of Reference for Languages: Learning, Teaching, Assessment.* Companion Volume with New Descriptors (Language Policy Programme Education Policy Division Education Department No. February). https://rm.coe.int/cefr-companion-volume-with-new-descriptors-2018/1680787989

European Parliament. (2006). *Recommendations of the European Parliament and Council on key competences for lifelong learning*. Official Journal of the European Union. https://eur-lex.europa.eu/legal-content/EN/TXT/PDF/?uri=CELEX:32006H0962&from=EN

Ferrari, A. (2013). *DigComp: a framework for developing and understanding digital competence in Europe*. Edited by Y. Punie & B. N. Brecko. Joint research centre, European Commission. https://doi.org/10.2788/52966

Hauck, M., & Kurek, M. (2017). Language and technology. In S. Thorne & S. May (Eds), *Language, education and technology, encyclopedia of language and education* (pp. 1-13). Springer International Publishing. https://doi.org/10.1007/978-3-319-02328-1

Ivankova, N. V. (2014). *Mixed methods applications in action research: from methods to community action*. SAGE Publications.

Klein, S. R. (2012). *Action research methods: plain and simple*. Palgrave Macmillan. https://doi.org/10.1057/9781137046635

Punie, Y., & Redecker, C. (2017). *Proposal for a European framework for the digital competence of educators. (DigCompEdu)*. European Commission.

Putman, S. M., & Rock, T. C. (2017). *Action research: using strategic inquiry to improve teaching and learning*. SAGE Publication.

UNESCO. (2008). *ICT competency standards for teachers: policy framework. UNESCO Archives*. https://unesdoc.unesco.org/ark:/48223/pf0000156210

UNESCO. (2011). *UNESCO ICT competency framework for teachers*. https://unesdoc.unesco.org/ark:/48223/pf0000213475

UNESCO. (2015). *Qingdao declaration*. Quindao. https://unesdoc.unesco.org/ark:/48223/pf0000233352

Vuorikari, R., Punie, Y., Carretero, S., & Van Den Brande, L. (2016). *DigComp 2.0: The Digital Competence Framework for Citizens. Update Phase 1: The Conceptual Reference Model*. European Commission. https://ec.europa.eu/jrc/en/publication/eur-scientific-and-technical-research-reports/digcomp-20-digital-competence-framework-citizens-update-phase-1-conceptual-reference-model

5. The EUniTA project: working with international partners to develop language, intercultural, and professional competencies in European university students

Sonia Cunico[1]

Abstract

Language tandem exchanges offer students valuable opportunities for autonomous learning and authentic intercultural communication encounters. This paper will discuss the key principles of tandem language exchange, and in particular online ones, and then present the EU-funded European University Tandem (EUniTa) project which was developed by colleagues from seven European partner universities to create an integrated online platform, with audio/video and chat interfaces. EUniTa allows an innovative automatic matching and meets the learning needs of university students by providing them with materials to develop their Basic Interpersonal Communication Skills (BICS) as well as their Cognitive Academic Language Proficiency (CALP). In the conclusion, areas for future research are identified to measure the success of the project and its longevity.

Keywords: language tandem exchange, collaborative learning, EUniTA, autonomy.

1. University of Exeter, Exeter, England; s.cunico@exeter.ac.uk

How to cite this chapter: Cunico, S. (2019). The EUniTA project: working with international partners to develop language, intercultural, and professional competencies in European university students. In C. Goria, L. Guetta, N. Hughes, S. Reisenleutner & O. Speicher (Eds), *Professional competencies in language learning and teaching* (pp. 53-64). Research-publishing.net. https://doi.org/10.14705/rpnet.2019.34.914

Chapter 5

1. Introduction

In the last 40 years language pedagogy has seen a major shift from being teacher-led and focussed on grammar and vocabulary to a more student-centred approach with a strong emphasis on communicative competence and autonomous learning. In addition, new technologies are increasingly playing a key role in breaking down geographical, temporal, social, and language barriers by allowing instant communication around the globe and offering students opportunities for authentic language use in meaningful social contexts. Globalisation is also having an impact on the UK higher education agenda, which places increasing importance on internationalisation and the development of graduates' intercultural competence to enable them to join a multilingual and multicultural working environment. In this context, this paper describes an Erasmus+ funded European Universities Language Tandem (EUniTa, https://www.eunita.org/) scheme designed to connect students across Europe and enable them to develop their language and intercultural competencies. It will discuss the rationale for its creation, its pedagogical underpinning and major outcomes so far, and also identify a number of areas which will need empirical research.

2. EUniTa: a 21st century university tandem language learning scheme

Calvert (1992, p. 17) defined tandem learning as a *reciprocal* learning scheme in which native speakers of two different languages work together to improve their language skills and their understanding of each other's culture. As a form of peer learning, students interact in an informal learning context (Funk, Gerlach, & Spaniel-Weise, 2017; Karjalainen, Pörn, Rusk, & Björkskog, 2013; Stickler & Lewis, 2003). Brammerts (1996, cited in Woodin, 2018, pp. 9-10) argues that tandem learning is based upon three underlying principles:

- **Autonomy.** you are responsible for your own learning. Tandem learners are responsible for identifying their own needs, setting their own goals, and finding the means to achieve them.

- **Reciprocity**: you are responsible for ensuring mutual benefits. Both partners have a responsibility towards each other to help each other learn so that they benefit equally from the exchange.

- **Intercultural learning**: as learning in tandem is based upon communication between members of different language-speaking communities and cultures, it also facilitates cultural learning.

The importance of exposure to the target language as well as to opportunities to produce language output is well recognised in research (Swain, 1985) and also by language teachers and students who value the possibility of interacting with native speakers of the language they are studying. Many university foreign language centres have long organised tandem language exchanges to allow students the possibility to practice their foreign language skills. There are many tandem language schemes: at one end of the spectrum there are some which are a compulsory component of a language module, fully integrated into the syllabus and with assessed learning outcomes – such as the one described by Morley and Truscott (2001, 2003) in which students must work in pairs to complete some tasks. At the other end, there are others which are totally independent from structured credit-bearing language modules, and they can also be organised autonomously by students. What all tandem language schemes have in common is that they create social contexts in which genuine communicative needs arise equally for both participants, and language learning is socially motivated and socially-mediated (Lantolf, 2000). Increasingly, social media play a key role in both managing and advertising the schemes. For instance, at Exeter University, we manage a Facebook page (with 1,792 followers) as a platform for students to autonomously contact potential tandem partners to set up face to face language exchanges, and also to advertise monthly social events, which are attended by up to 50 students at a time.

However, a common problem in university tandem schemes is the large imbalance in supply and demand for certain native speaker combinations and organisers of tandem schemes in language centres are familiar with the scenario of not being able to meet home students' aspirations with the linguistic human resources available at a local level. This is a great cause of dissatisfaction and frustration among students who cannot benefit from the scheme.

Since the 1990s, various technologies have offered the possibility of setting up transnational tandem schemes to resolve the imbalance between L1/L2 demands. Early examples are the exchanges coordinated by Helmut Brammerts of the Ruhr-Universitat Bochum with what he calls a network of 'bilingual subnets' for tandem learning using the internet (Brammerts & Little, 1996) and more recently collaborative learning through Japanese-Spanish tele-tandem (González & Nagao, 2018). Such schemes are normally not available to all undergraduate students since they tend to be set up by individual teachers for their own students at the participating universities, thus limiting wider participation. In addition, since they often lack major institutional investment, they tend to rely on specific individuals' initiatives, contacts with colleagues in other foreign institutions, and use of their own time to set them up. As a result, such schemes can be short-lived.

A quick internet search reveals that there are now a number of language tandem platforms and apps which students can access (see https://europa.eu/youth/eu/article/54/42957_en_en for a list of tandem websites and apps). However, they are not necessarily suitable for higher education students: some of them appear to provide tandem matching as part of a private language learning business. They also lack institutional credentials and safety checks, and it is therefore problematic to vouch for their appropriateness for our students. Often, they present the tandem experience as unproblematic and seem deliberately oblivious to the challenges that online tandems present to their users, such as having the ability of identifying one's own needs and means to achieve them, or finding the right match in terms of one's needs (level of language competence, aspirations, time available, etc.):

> "[a] conversation exchange or tandem is quite simple: if you speak French and want to brush up your Greek, for instance, you'll need to find a Greek partner who is learning French" (http://europa.eu/youth/eu/article/54/42957_en).

Since matching is a common problem in higher education across Europe, it was clear that there was potential to make full use of modern technologies to develop a very flexible open educational resource able to match tandem university peers transnationally and to create authentic communicative contexts for pairs of native speakers of different languages. The EUniTa project was the product of an international collaboration which developed out of the need to find a long-term solution to a shared local problem. The project was financially supported by the European Union under the Erasmus+ Programme between October 2015 and April 2019 and involved seven partner universities from five European countries – University of Exeter, University of Florence, Goethe University Frankfurt, University of Liverpool, Paris Sorbonne University, University of Poitiers, and Blanquerna, University Ramon Llull.

The unique and distinctive features of EUniTa are its dedicated and self-contained online platform accessible to any EU student who can, at the click of a finger, sign up for a tandem language exchange, get matched automatically, and find the necessary communication tools as well learning resources they may need *within* the platform itself (Figure 1).

Figure 1. EUniTa is designed as a desktop application which can be used on tablets and smartphones

Chapter 5

3. The creation of a virtual social space for a professional transnational learning community

Based on new web real-time communications technology, the EUniTa platform (hosted by the University of Frankfurt) is designed to match large numbers of tandem learners without a time consuming registration and matching process. One of the greatest strengths of EUniTA is its simplicity of use and wide availability: it has been developed as an open source online tandem platform designed for multiple electronic devices including computers, tablet computers, or smartphones, and is able to connect students nearly instantaneously.

Figure 2. Quick online registration which allows instant access to tandem matches

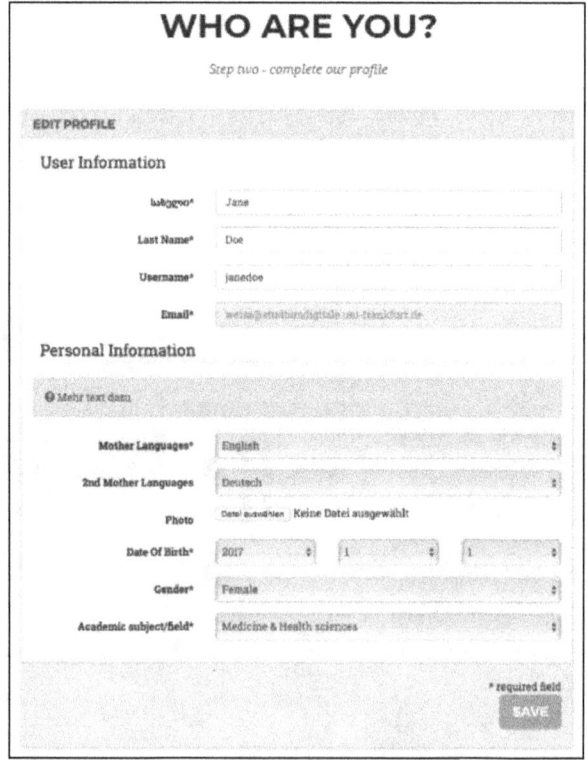

The online registration form (Figure 2) was designed taking into account a survey of approximately 500 students from all partner intuitions: it is user friendly with quick and short questions which aim to build the students' profile (age, gender, and academic discipline). Once registered the matching is automatic and students can start their tandem exchange experience straightaway.

The EUniTa platform allows students to have multiple exchanges at the same time, and to be in touch by instant messaging or audio and video chat, and to access and share supporting material tailor-made to their language competence should they need it. It also allows students to monitor their progress, and receive a certificate of participation in the tandem exchange (Figure 3), issued by their home university.

Figure 3. The EUniTa dashboard provides an overview of all the tools, activities, and material available on the platform

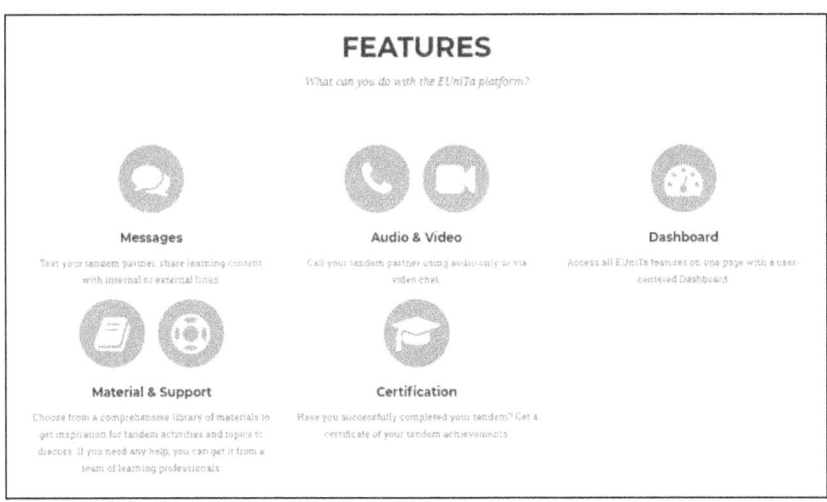

Since disciplinary matching is enabled, EUniTa allows students to develop their Basic Interpersonal Conversation Skills (BICS) as well as their Cognitive Academic Language Proficiency (CALP). Although the meaning of the terms have varied, the main distinction refers to "the extent to which the meaning being communicated is supported by contextual or interpersonal cues (such as gestures, facial expressions, and intonation present in face-to-face interaction) or dependent on linguistic cues that are largely independent of the immediate communicative context" (Cumming, 2014, p. 3).

The EUniTa library stores tailor made resources which aim to support the development of BICS: they are easily identifiable both in terms of content (society, daily life, studies and careers, health, sports, etc.) and in terms of levels of language proficiency based on the Common European Framework of Reference for languages. The resources aim to generate discussion on students' lives, their values, and cultural practices, and by exposing them to their differences increase their intercultural awareness. When completing the registration, students can choose to provide information about their academic subject and be matched with a student from a similar academic field. The aim of this innovative feature is to support CALP, the development of a cognitively demanding language which is subject specific, relates to abstract concepts, has specialised vocabulary, and uses more complex language structures, as well as discipline specific practices such as discussing and evaluating data and reports. Students may have sufficient language competence to operate effectively in everyday situations, but they may have limited opportunities to develop CALP sufficiently well to function in a professional environment. In fact, although students may have encountered formal language used in their field of studies, it may have been decontextualised or in written texts only, disconnected from the professional practices it inhabits. With the exception of the time spent abroad studying at a partner institution, normally students have very few opportunities to use subject specific terminology and discuss discipline specific issues in a really communicative context with a native speaker of their L2.

The following screenshot provides an overview of the range of discipline-specific material and activities available on the platform (Figure 4 below).

The purpose of the CALP section is to support meaningful and purposeful encounters between L1/L2 students with common discipline backgrounds. In this way, it is hoped that EUnITA may facilitate student agency by fostering online socialising processes based on common expertise and professional interests, whereby learners are able to co-construct contexts in which expertise and knowledge is shared among participants.

Figure 4. CALP resources and tasks available on EUniTa

Titel	Level	Prep.	Language			
Defining key terms	B2	Yes	Deutsch	English	Español	Italiano
Debating	B2	No	Deutsch	English	Español	Italiano
Talking about books	C1	No	Deutsch	English	Español	
Field interviews	B2	No	Deutsch	English	Español	Italiano
Discussions and predictions	B2	No	Deutsch	English	Español	Italiano
Pitching and negotiating	B2	No	Deutsch	English	Español	Italiano
Presenting research interests	B2	No	Deutsch	English	Español	Italiano
Posters and presentations	B2,C1	No	Deutsch	English	Español	Italiano
Research areas	B1,B2	No	Deutsch	English	Español	Italiano
Research methodology and presentations	B2	No	Deutsch	English	Español	Italiano
Research questions and implications	B2	No	Deutsch	English	Español	Italiano
Surveys	B2	No	Deutsch	English	Español	Italiano

(Social Sciences, Economics & Law)

4. Conclusion

EUniTa is now completed and will soon be ready to be used by students from all the seven original partner institutions. It will also be open to any other universities who wish to join for a small fee by signing the EUniTa consortium agreement.

Although EU funding has now come to an end, ongoing research will be needed to measure EUnITa's future success and potential limitations. Firstly, on a practical level, it will be important to verify if EUniTa has been able to successfully resolve the local matching problem and shortage of L1/L2 native speakers for certain language combinations. The EUniTA set up and resources are presently available only in the languages of the original partner institutions (Catalan, English, French, German, Italian, and Spanish, so the participation of other European partners will be required to increase the pool of potential L1/L2 matches. Also, given that Asian languages have increased their popularity at A-level and undergraduate level, the possibility of opening up EUniTa to non-EU universities will have to be explored in the very near future to allow students the possibility to be matched with languages such as Chinese, Korean, or Japanese.

Secondly, research will be needed to test whether, and *how*, students use the online resources made available on the platform, *if* the resources provide a helpful structure to frame students' tandem exchanges or if students prefer and are able to negotiate the terms and objectives of the tandem totally autonomously. In the latter case, future research should explore how students mobilise autonomy and co-dependence in the tandem scheme.

Thirdly, the CALP resources were developed to facilitate the development of discipline specific language competence and skills, and research will be needed to measure students' interest in CALP and, looking further ahead, the degree to which CALP matching has supported the development of professional networks and long term relationships amongst transnational graduates.

Fourthly, it will be important to quantify the longevity of electronic tandem matches to see how long they endure when they are not integrated into an institutional framework, or set up and managed by a tutor who maintains some degree of authority and control over the scheme and matches. Brammerts (1995) identified autonomy and reciprocity as important principles for the success of tandem schemes, and research will be needed to verify the extent to which students commit themselves to the tandem exchange and/or if the simplicity of registration and matching make their commitment and investment short lived in this era of casual internet-based encounters.

Finally, while locally organised tandem schemes depend on enthusiastic staff setting them up and maintaining them, EUniTa will depend on its success and future existence on the financial support of the institutions which are part of the consortium to meet the costs involved in the maintenance of the EUniTa digital infrastructure. In making a case for ongoing financial support, it will be important to be able to articulate, with empirical evidence, how EUniTa supports language learning and intercultural competence, which are part of many higher institutions' internationalisation agendas. Similarly, we need to demonstrate how, in a context in which English is currently the dominant European *lingua franca*, EUniTa can support the development of multilingual graduates with an international outlook in a socio-political environment which is at times divisive and increasingly problematic in terms of the reinforcement of national identity and boundaries.

Acknowledgements

I would like to thank the European Union funding for the EUniTa project as part of the Erasmus+ Programme, as well as our project partners and the students involved in testing and providing feedback on the platform development. I would also like to thank the two reviewers who have provided me with helpful comments.

References

Brammerts, H. (1995). Tandem learning and the Internet. Using new technology to acquire intercultural competence. *Intercultural competence: a new challenge for language teachers and trainers in Europe, 2*, 209-222.

Brammerts, H. (1996). Language learning in tandem using the internet. In *Telecollaboration in Foreign Language Learning: Proceedings of the Hawai'i Symposium* (pp. 121-130). University of Hawai's Second language Teaching Center.

Brammerts, H., & Little, D. (Eds). (1996). A guide to language learning in tandem via the internet. *Preface CLCS Occasional Paper, 46*.

Calvert, M. (1992). Working in tandem: peddling an old idea. *Language Learning Journal, 6*(1), 17-19. https://doi.org/10.1080/09571739285200371

Cumming, J. (2014). Basic interpersonal communicative skills and cognitive academic language proficiency. https://www.researchgate.net/publication/242539680_Basic_ Interpersonal_Communicative_Skills_and_Cognitive_Academic_Language_Proficiency

Funk, H., Gerlach, M., & Spaniel-Weise, D. (Eds). (2017). *Handbook for foreign language learning in online tandems and educational settings*. Peter Lang. https://doi.org/10.3726/b10732

González, S., & Nagao, K. (2018). Collaborative learning through Japanese-Spanish teletandem. *Studies in self-access learning journal, 9*(2), 196-216.

Karjalainen, K., Pörn, M., Rusk, F., & Björkskog, L. (2013). Classroom tandem-outlining a model for language learning and instruction. *Electronic Journal of Elementary Education, 6*(1), 165-184. https://www.pegem.net/dosyalar/dokuman/138603-2014010816593-9.pdf

Lantolf, J. P. (2000). *Socio-cultural theory and second language learning*. Oxford University Press.

Morley, J., & Truscott, S. (2001). Setting up a credit-rated tandem scheme. In M. Mozzon-McPherson & R. Vismans (Eds), *Beyond language teaching towards language advising* (pp.199-208). CILT.

Morley, J., & Truscott, S. (2003). The integration of research-oriented learning into a tandem learning programme. *The language Learning Journal, 27*(1), 52-58. https://doi.org/10.1080/09571730385200081

Stickler, U., & Lewis, T. (2003). Tandem learning and intercultural competence. In T. Lewis & L. Walker (Eds), *Language learning in tandem* (pp. 93-104). Academy Electronic Publications.

Swain, M. (1985). Communicative competence: some roles of comprehensible input and comprehensible output in its development. In S. Gass & C. Madden (Eds), *Input in second language acquisition*, (pp. 165-179).

Woodin, J. (2018). *Interculturality, interaction and language learning: insights from tandem partnerships*. Routledge. https://doi.org/10.4324/9781315640525

6. Integrating the language aspects of intercultural competencies into language for specific purposes programmes

Zita Hajdu[1] and Renáta Domonyi[2]

Abstract

Business schools and their foreign language departments are expected to support their students in the transition from the academic sphere into the world of work, where non-domain skills including intercultural competencies have gained importance in degree jobs. To react to labour market trends, the Institute of Business Communication and Professional Language Studies decided to offer courses of intercultural skills with the aim of preparing students for appropriate and effective communication in an international environment. This is to be achieved by developing open, conscious, and adaptable behaviour and also by the acquisition of the linguistic and non-language elements of intercultural communication. Students should know how information is conveyed both in their mother tongue and the target language (explicit and subtle ways of expressing thoughts, potential areas of misunderstanding). The paper also deals with the benefits business organisations can gain by possessing intercultural competencies.

Keywords: intercultural skills, labour market, translation, effective communication.

---

1. University of Debrecen, Debrecen, Hungary; hajdu.zita@econ.unideb.hu

2. University of Debrecen, Debrecen, Hungary; domonyi.renata@econ.unideb.hu

How to cite this chapter: Hajdu, Z., & Domonyi, R. (2019). Integrating the language aspects of intercultural competencies into language for specific purposes programmes. In C. Goria, L. Guetta, N. Hughes, S. Reisenleutner & O. Speicher (Eds), *Professional competencies in language learning and teaching* (pp. 65-75). Research-publishing.net. https://doi.org/10.14705/rpnet.2019.34.915

1. Introduction

A marked characteristic of the current labour market is the increasing need for adaptable competencies. Apart from the desired qualification, employers require universal, non-domain competencies that are not specific to certain jobs. Intercultural skills form part of the selection process in an indirect way, often as part of complex assignments. Furthermore, a lot of students aspire to undertake scholarships or research work abroad. These trends have inspired the Institute to launch courses in intercultural competencies with the aim of enabling students to study or work efficiently in a multinational environment. At the Faculty of Economics and Business, Debrecen University, intercultural studies and skills are part of the Business English programme at Bachelor of the Arts (BA) and Bachelor of Science (BSc) level, and as independent subjects they are taught at master level. A shorter programme for science students of other faculties (*Intercultural skills for science students at master level*) and two more complex subjects (*Intercultural studies for technical translators* and *Intercultural language skills for translators*) for technical translators of business have been designed. When compiling the content of the courses, research results and human resources experts' experience have both been considered.

2. Intercultural competencies in the labour market

The growth of soft skills, e.g. global citizenship, professional ethics, problem solving, or team work was predicted by a business research organisation, DeakinCo (2017) who carried out their research among key industry experts. According to this forecast, soft skill-intensive occupations will have accounted for two thirds of all jobs and soft skill intensive jobs will have grown 2.5 times faster than other jobs by 2030 (DeakinCo, 2017).

Due to the growing significance of cultural factors affecting the quality of the relationship between economic players, there has been a shift towards non-economic factors, e.g. intercultural competences (Fornalska & Skurczynski, 2014).

According to Bhawuk and Brislin (1992), intercultural sensitivity can predetermine an individual's ability to work efficiently with people from other cultures. They state that people must be interested in other cultures and out of respect to these cultures they have to adapt or modify their behaviour. The affective aspect of intercultural sensitivity, the cognitive aspect of intercultural awareness and the behavioural aspect of intercultural effectiveness as described by Chen and Starosta (1996) are of special importance when we prepare our students for the challenges of the future labour market.

Cross-cultural competencies serve the interest of recent graduates in finding a job as these skills are beneficial for the organisations which employ them. Customer satisfaction and customer loyalty generate company success, and these goals cannot be reached without smooth and effective communication with the clients. This includes the clear wording of contracts, the accurate comprehension and completion of orders, and first of all building and maintaining relationships through amiable negotiations, which all require a thorough knowledge of other cultures (Thitthongkam, Walsh, & Banchapattanasakda, 2010).

Finding the financial and business benefits of possessing cross-cultural communication competencies was the aim of an extensive survey involving more than 300 big companies on four continents and identified the following yields:

- acquiring new customers through openness to and respect for other cultures,

- a better understanding of differing viewpoints and ways of thinking,

- improved handling of conflicts,

- more effective teamwork, and

- growing trust in the company and thus enhanced reputation.

Adaptation to different cultural settings and adjusting discourse accordingly, furthermore, being aware of one's own cultural biases and conduct were also mentioned as important (British Council, 2013). In an earlier research project conducted by the EU on the financial gains of having foreign language and intercultural skills, numerical benefits and losses were targeted, and 18 percent of the questioned business organisations identified cooperation problems due to cultural differences and misunderstandings (Hagen et al., 2006).

3. Curriculum for intercultural courses

3.1. Curriculum goals

The desired outcome of the subject is borrowed from Deardorff's (2006) intercultural competence model: to communicate effectively and appropriately in an intercultural situation using one's intercultural knowledge, skills, and attitudes. Ideally students develop empathy, adaptability, and consciousness. Regarding attitude, the key words of training are respect and openness. In the one semester master programme for science students, the aim is to clarify culture specific language points, for example the choice of words, ways of expressing oneself, and style of writing. Furthermore, students should also be aware of the differences in behaviour and attitude.

The faculty also offers a four semester programme for technical translators which involves a subject of intercultural studies and another subject for intercultural language skills. The purpose of teaching intercultural studies for would-be translators is providing them with the key drivers in native speakers' way of thinking appearing in communication. For example, when the love of freedom and democracy appears in the language in the form of offering the speaker several choices to express his way of looking at things, this is new to an Eastern European student. The *Intercultural language skills for translators* course involves more sophisticated issues as well, such as the confident application of associations, connotations, and transmission of political views with minimal loss in meaning.

3.2. Content elements of the curriculum

3.2.1. Intercultural skills for science students at master level

Based on the above mentioned consideration points, the following curriculum has been compiled for master students of natural sciences.

Non-language elements:

- cultures (definition, components, characteristics, classifications);

- intercultural communication ethics (awareness, respect, empathy, tolerance);

- major attitude themes (time, punctuality, degrees of politeness, formality, being open);

- non-verbal intercultural communication (gestures, mimics, eye-contact, the value of silence, dress code); and

- potential areas of intercultural conflicts.

Most students are aware that political views and religious beliefs should be avoided in a business conversation but they need to be warned of some further dangerous topics, such as ethnic jokes or country-sensitive historic or military topics. Learning the cultural roots of certain patterns of behaviour or attitudes helps to remember them, as in the saying 'consider the past, you'll know the present'.

Students are especially interested in the life of their peers in other cultures or the way they are learning foreign languages. As European teenagers prefer learning through 'user experiences' they are always surprised at the strict or sometimes rigid way Japanese schoolchildren study. Glossary booklets teaching foreign language words with translations and example sentences to be memorised have always been fashionable in Japan. Europeans would probably find this method of learning too boring (Szirmai & Czellér, 2014).

Linguistic parts in the curriculum:

- differences between high and low context languages;
- ways of keeping or altering reality;
- emotional or rational, sometimes flowery, ways of speaking;
- short or long ways of expressing thoughts;
- taboos in conversation, ethnic jokes;
- ways of asking, requesting;
- degrees of directness;
- degrees of loudness;
- the importance of small talks;
- the language of numbers – trillion, billion, decimal point; and
- units of measurement.

When we introduce a culture from the aspect of the language, first of all we need to tell whether it is an explicit or subtle language. Do they say what they think or does the listener have to decode the meaning because part of the message is hidden?

As English is a lingua franca which is used for communication between non-native speakers as well, speakers of English should also be aware of the peculiarities of cultures outside the Anglo-Saxon world. Without background information, one might not understand them or misunderstandings may occur. Apart from the typical British understatement, native speakers of English tend to speak in a straightforward, direct way to avoid misunderstandings and uncertainties. When they give information it is explicit, concrete, detailed, but at the same time accurate. When classifying cultures, one can establish that native speakers of English are more unambiguous than for example Asian people with their very polite sentences or Mexicans with their diminutives. However, examining different areas of the Anglo-Saxon world one can notice differences in the way of speaking and this requires careful interpretation. To correctly understand British speakers we need to know that politeness is a key concept in British language and culture and this leads to nicer ways of wording things, very often in the form of euphemisms and understatements. Due to this, intonation and mimicry gain special importance. We all know how many different meanings the word *interesting* can convey.

Paying attention to the intonation and being conscious about the special characteristics of a language can support appropriate interpretation. The same refers to the various meanings of the word *yes* in the Japanese language. All this shows that the introduction of high and low context cultures needs to be an essential part of the curriculum. Students should know if the language they study conveys meaning through codes or context, or how precise information giving is. The most important point is how direct or straightforward speakers are or if the listener has to guess or deduct background information. If we look at the items in the Anglo-EU Translation Guide (Table 1), we can see that most of them are exaggerations, but that is why students will surely remember them and learn that in some cultures they cannot interpret utterances literally. In employment situations, serious misunderstandings or conflicts may arise from being unaware of the secondary or hidden meanings of phrases or statements.

Table 1. Anglo-EU translation guide[3]

What the British say	What the British mean	What others understand
You must come for dinner	It's not an invitation. I am just being polite	I will get an invitation soon
I almost agree	I don't agree at all	He's not far from agreement
I only have a few minor comments	Please re-write it completely	He has found a few typos
Could we consider some other options?	I don't like your idea	They have not yet decided
I will bear it in mind	I've forgotten it already	They will probably do it
Very interesting	That is clearly nonsense	They are impressed
I was a bit disappointed that...	I am annoyed that	It doesn't really matter
That's not bad	That's good	That's poor
I am sure it's my fault	It's your fault	Why do they think it was their fault?

3. https://www.reddit.com/r/CasualUK/comments/80kskd/angloeu_translation_guide/

3.2.2. Intercultural studies for technical translators

The Faculty of Economics and Business offers a master programme for would-be translators of economics and business who are at C1 level (Common European Framework of Reference) when starting the two-year-course with 644 contact hours and a complex final exam. This programme involves two subjects of intercultural communication: a theoretical one called *Intercultural studies for technical translators*, and a more practical one entitled *Intercultural language skills for technical translators*. The list below includes those topics which are not taught in the non-translation courses. These are mainly management issues: intercultural differences and conflicts in management.

Course elements:

- interrelationships between organisational and national cultures in multinational companies;

- cultural diversity in management; and

- globalisation and localisation.

3.2.3. Intercultural language skills for technical translators

Students of the technical translation course are all Business and Economics majors, and they have only studied the major events and trends in English or American history, civilisation or English-American literature and culture. Due to this, they need to get familiar with a lot of words and phrases whose meanings are rooted in the culture of the target language. These can be everyday words like *brunch, shawl, patio*, or *bungalow* or political words like *the Tories, the Blitz* or *the establishment*, or words from the world of sport such as *to touch base with someone*.

Course content (exclusively the extra topics compared to the non-translation courses):

- linguistic characteristics of professional communication (formality) in the source and target language; and

- culture specific words, phrases grouped by topic.

3.2.4. Intercultural aspects in translation strategies

Intercultural aspects in translation strategies do not form an independent subject in the translation teaching programme, but it is an important factor in the training of translators. From an intercultural point of view, the starting point for a translator is what he considers more determining: the similarities or differences of cultures. The next factor is what he regards primary: the text of the source language or that of the target language. Another significant point when evaluating translation is that one cannot have the same expectations of the source and the target language, as the background knowledge and the intentions of the creator, the translator, and the recipient are different. Furthermore, having the same impact as the source text cannot be the only criterion of a good translation, because the translation itself is only one of many factors (age, educational level, geographical location, etc.) influencing reception (Nida, 2000). Nida (2000) states that a good translator should equally be familiar with the culture and the language of the source and the target languages, as words can only convey meaning together with their cultural background. He also emphasises that the differences between the two cultures may generate more challenges for the translator than the differing language structures. This statement may sound like an exaggeration but it should be accepted that a thorough knowledge of the source and the target culture is a key factor in translation.

4. Conclusion

Intercultural competencies are key skills in translation and also in other degree-level jobs, and it is the role of the higher education institutions to prepare students for intercultural tasks arising in their studies or future work. Raising consciousness by highlighting the differences in cultures and the consequences of ignoring them should be the first step of the teacher. Although the general aims of intercultural competency courses are the same, different curriculum content is needed for the training of translators and master students of science or business. Would-be translators need sophisticated knowledge of the cultures they are working with. Although company managers and human resource experts helped with the course design, an on-going development of the course content is needed to include new phenomena and expectations of the labour market and the experience of recent graduates. Because of this, a survey is being planned to receive feedback from former students who are employed in organisations with international activity.

References

Bhawuk, D. P., & Brislin, R. (1992). The measurement of intercultural sensitivity using the concepts of individualism and collectivism. *International journal of intercultural relations, 16*(4), 413-436. https://doi.org/10.1016/0147-1767(92)90031-O

British Council. (2013). *Culture at work: the value of intercultural skills in the workplace.* http://www.britishcouncil.org/sites/britishcouncil.uk2/files/culture-at-work-report-v2.pdf

Chen, G. M., & Starosta, W. J. (1996). Intercultural communication competence: a synthesis. *Annals of the International Communication Association, 19*(1), 353-383. https://doi.org/10.1080/23808985.1996.11678935

DeakinCo. (2017). *Soft skills for business success.* https://www2.deloitte.com/content/dam/Deloitte/au/Documents/Economics/deloitte-au-economics-deakin-soft-skills-business-success-170517.pdf

Deardorff, D. K. (2006). Identification and assessment of intercultural competence as a student outcome of internationalization. *Journal of studies in international education, 10*(3), 241-266. https://doi.org/10.1177/1028315306287002

Fornalska, A., & Skurczyński, M. (2014). Intercultural competence of employees as a non-economic factor influencing competitiveness in the international market. *International Business and Global Economy, 33,* 543-554. https://doi.org/10.4467/23539496IB.13.040.2425

Hagen, S., Foreman-Peck, J., Davila-Philippon, S., Nordgren, B., & Hagen, S. (2006). *ELAN: effects on the European economy of shortages of foreign language skills in enterprise.* The UK National Centre for Languages (CiLT).

Nida, E. (2000). Principles of correspondence. 1964. *Bassnet, Susan. Translation Studies.*

Szirmai, M., & Czellér, M. (2014). Hagyományos szótanulás modern eszközökkel. *Nyelv, társadalom, kultúra: interkulturális és multikulturális perpektívá, 1-2,*(23). Magyar Alkalmazott Nyelvészeti Kongresszus, 400.

Thitthongkam, T., Walsh, J., & Banchapattanasakda, C. (2010). The roles of foreign language in business administration. *Journal of Management Research, 3*(1), 1-15. https://doi.org/10.5296/jmr.v3i1.509

7. Teaching intercultural competencies at the University of Debrecen

Ildikó Tar[1] and Tímea Lázár[2]

Abstract

The education of intercultural competencies and the related skills are at the forefront of teaching at Debrecen University. The teaching materials are based on the work of esteemed authors like Hofstede, Hall, and Trompenaars. However, new cultural and social realities evolve, and educators of intercultural communication need to be responsive to these changes. The article discusses recent surveys carried out by the Budapest College of Communication, Business, and Arts in Budapest in 2004-2012 and SCOPE Intercultural Communication Services LLC (of which the first author is a member) in 2007-2017 on the transformation of the typical features in Hungarian culture, using Hofstede's (1983) original four indices and some additional ones developed by Hall and Hall (1990) and Smith, Dugan, and Trompenaars (1996). The study compares these findings with Hofstede's (1983) corresponding results on Hungary. The authors have found significant differences between the two sets of results and attempted to identify the underlying causes. The paper emphasises the significance of these new findings in raising intercultural awareness in Hungary and Europe in the global framework, and use them as a basis for teaching intercultural competencies through language learning for students.

Keywords: Hofstede, Hungarian survey, cultural differences, underlying causes, intercultural awareness.

---

1. University of Debrecen, Debrecen, Hungary; ildikotar@econ.unideb.hu

2. University of Debrecen, Debrecen, Hungary; lazar.timea@econ.unideb.hu

How to cite this chapter: Tar, I., & Lázár, T. (2019). Teaching intercultural competencies at the University of Debrecen. In C. Goria, L. Guetta, N. Hughes, S. Reisenleutner & O. Speicher (Eds), *Professional competencies in language learning and teaching* (pp. 77-88). Research-publishing.net. https://doi.org/10.14705/rpnet.2019.34.916

Chapter 7

1. Introduction

As with globalisation, the spread of multinational companies and the enormous development of information technology can lead to a new trend in employers' requirements, and formal education and foreign language teaching have an important role in improving intercultural competencies. These competencies can be learned and activated in the classroom and can be improved at the workplace. According to Fantini and Tirmizi's (2006) definition, intercultural competence refers to complex capabilities which are needed to be able to communicate effectively and appropriately when we interact with people culturally and linguistically different from us. Intercultural skills and competencies are present in a new European Union initiative whose aim is to help communication across Europe when it comes to working, learning, and training between different nations (European Commission, 2017). European Skills, Competencies, Qualifications, and Occupations is a multilingual classification system for European qualifications, occupations skills, and competencies.

When teaching intercultural competencies, the first step is help students explore and gain comfort with their own cultural identity. This will help them become open to explore other cultures different than their own and leads to gaining intercultural competency. The authors took the deliberate decision to outline Hofstede's (1983) model, identify his rankings on Hungary, and carry out a new survey in the specific circumstances of Hungarian culture, which yielded somewhat different results about four decades later. The study seeks to explore the potential underlying reasons behind the two sets of findings and provides a plausible explanation for the discrepancies. Throughout its history, Hungary has almost always been a kind of buffer state and a battlefield between east and west over the centuries of European history (Molnár, 2001). This role of Hungary aroused the authors' interest in establishing new understandings of Hungarian mentality, thinking, and awareness of its specific cultural features. Hungarian culture may be characterised by a unique integration of eastern and western cultures, e.g. the Ottoman rule of 150 years (16th and 17th centuries), or the Habsburg dominance of 230 years and the impact of the French enlightenment in the 18th century, to mention two particular examples from recent times. The results of these influences can be summarised as follows according to Hungarian psychologist Margot Honti: Hungarians are typically receptive to cultural influences, they show readiness to learn new methods and technologies, they show passive resistance against oppression, and always find out how they can cunningly overcome problems in whatever circumstances (in Falkné Bánó, 2002, p. 64). Hungarians are usually considered to be pessimistic but seem to have a brilliant sense of humour, which translates into sarcasm and smart jokes. The present situation of Hungary is similarly characterised by multiple external influences such as the process of globalisation, the changes of the world economy, and the conflicting policies of European and global powers. Several authors have attempted to explore the typical Hungarian mentality and mindset. Honti claims that "Hungarians have lost self-esteem on the outside, but this nation is very, very proud in its depths" (cited in Falkné Bánó, 2002, p. 64). Another expert on the subject, László Honti further notes that "[a] lack of outward aggressiveness or assertiveness is coupled with a deep inner sense of pride and national identity" (cited in Falkné Bánó, 2002, p. 64). This context lends itself to fast changes and transformations as to how Hungarians react, behave, and think these days. The 2017 survey carried out by SCOPE Intercultural Communication Services LLC that will be discussed below used the somewhat modified and updated version of Hofstede's (2010) survey.

2. The concept of culture: Hofstede's (2011) model

First, the word *culture* was "used by [the] ancient Roman orator Cicero and he used it for the cultivation of the soul. Culture can be defined broadly, and it can affect many aspects of human life" (Lázár, 2017, p. 93). Alternatively, culture can be defined in a narrow sense referring to civilisation. Culture can be learned, and it is not the same as human nature or an individual's personality. Hofstede's (2011) definition of culture is: "[c]ulture is the collective programming of the mind that distinguishes the members of one group or category of people from others" (p. 3). Culture manifests itself in symbols, heroes, rituals, and values, and practices at different levels. In their book, Hofstede, Hofstede, and Minkov (2010) identified different layers of culture. Among these layers there is a

Chapter 7

national level according to one's country which implies that cultures may vary from country to country.

Hofstede (1983) had the opportunity to study the data collected at the subsidiaries in several countries of a large multinational company called International Business Machines (IBM). The respondents were matched groups of employees in seven occupational categories. The questionnaires were designed as a management tool and developed through open-ended pilot interviews (Hofstede, 2006). It is from this study that Hofstede (2006) found the following dimensions of cultures: power distance, collectivism versus individualism, femininity versus masculinity, and uncertainty avoidance. These four dimensions gave the model of differences among national cultures. To these four dimensions, two other dimensions were added later: long- versus short-term orientation and indulgence versus restraint (Hofstede et al., 2010). Long- versus short-term orientation correlates with some family values, school results, business and environmental values, and economic growth regarding national scores (Hofstede & Minkov, 2010). In Hofstede's (1983) model, each country is positioned on each empirically verifiable dimension in relation to other countries. In 2001, Van Oudenhoven examined the validity of Hofstede's (1983) classification of national cultures, and in his research, he found that the results considerably support Hofstede's (1983) four dimensions. Beugelsdijk, Maseland, and Van Hoorn (2015) examined how country scores have changed over time in Hofstede's (1983) dimensions. Bakir, Blodgett, Vitell, and Rose (2015) attempted to refine Hofstede's (1983) scales to be able to measure the culture's effect on marketing concepts.

Hofstede's (1983) scores have been used for many years in cultural research and in cross-cultural studies (Brewer & Venaik, 2011, 2012). The dimensions have been used in university courses and cross-cultural training programmes all over the world (Hofstede, 2010). Hofstede's (2010) model has proven to be a useful tool in global marketing and advertising. Cultural values play an important role in defining consumers' personalities. Companies with global brands want consumers to attribute the same brand personalities all over the world, but in fact, they can be influenced by their personal preferences. In different cultures, different interpersonal communication styles are interpreted in advertising. Hofstede's (2010) model can help companies understand differences in consumer behaviour across cultures (De Mooij & Hofstede, 2010).

Corey, Fok, and Payne (2014) examined cross-cultural differences in the cultural values and conflict handling styles, and they found that national origin and cultural values were decisive in two dimensions: individualism and long-term orientation.

Cultural differences can influence the perspective of whether a project is considered a success and the following dimensions are core "in valuing project success criteria: power distance, masculinity, uncertainty avoidance, [...] and long-term orientation" (Koops et al., 2015, p. 119). Altaf (2011) used Hofstede's (1983) four dimensions to assess how organisational culture can influence organisational effectiveness and his results showed that power distance has a negative impact on it, while collectivism has a positive impact.

For multinational companies, it is inevitable to improve their performance by the selection of the best composition of international and intercultural working groups. In a culturally diverse group, harmonising the behaviour and the actions of the individuals helps to achieve more effective performances, and national cultures of the individuals play a significant role. Small power distance, focus on short-term orientation, and indulgence influence task performance positively (Henning, 2016).

Organisational culture differences are composed of different elements compared to national cultural differences and can be defined at three levels: national, occupational, and organisational levels (Hofstede, Neuijen, Ohayv, & Sanders, 1990). They state that "[n]ational cultures and organisational cultures are phenomena of different orders: using the term 'cultures' for both is, in fact, somewhat misleading" (Hofstede et al., 1990, p. 313).

If companies want to change their culture, they can try to take some measures like enforcing a different company language, hiring or firing employees, or changing career advancement policies. Organisations should self-organise into these new patterns, and its realisation leads to cultural changes (Hofstede, 2015).

With his work, Hofstede (1980) could achieve the goal of making managers sensitive to cultural differences and providing a better basis for comparisons between cultures and organisations (Kieser, 1994).

3. The research

Survey 1. The Budapest College of Communication, Business, and Arts in Budapest carried out its Intercultural Awareness surveys in 2004-2012 with the participation of its student groups from all years and majors, typically with up to 60 students per group. The total number of respondents was 1,013. The College and Scope LLC have had regular cooperation in research activities on multicultural issues since 2009. With their kind permission, the authors could use their findings for analysis and comparison with the Scope results.

Survey 2. Scope LLC and the authors drew up a broader questionnaire on 'cultural dimensions' based on Hofstede's (1983) original one and supplemented it with four well-known dimensions: high context versus low context (Hall & Hall, 1990), long- versus short-term orientation (Hofstede et al., 1990), monochronic versus polychronic (Hall & Hall, 1990), and universalism versus particularism (Smith et al., 1996) in their research studies to adapt it to the Hungarian society.

One of the main activities of SCOPE LLC is the provision of training courses on intercultural sensitivity for companies, universities, and businesses. Scope LLC has surveyed 4,665 respondents in Hungary (students, training participants, company leaders, and staff members) usually 10-15 participants per training group in 2006-2017 (Scope, 2017). As noted above, the survey used by Scope is based on the original questionnaire by Hofstede (1983), but some more dimensions were added as well as some related questions indispensable for getting a special picture of the behavioural patterns of 21st century societies.

The first five sections of the survey include questions about an imaginary, ideal country and social community (I feel the best where...), whereas the other two sections are about actual life situations and individual preferences. A scale of one to five was used for the evaluation of responses and averages were calculated (Figure 1).

Figure 1. Intercultural Awareness survey 2004-2012, Budapest College of Communication, Business, and Arts in Budapest versus Intercultural sensitivity survey results (Scope, 2017, reproduced with kind permissions from Scope)

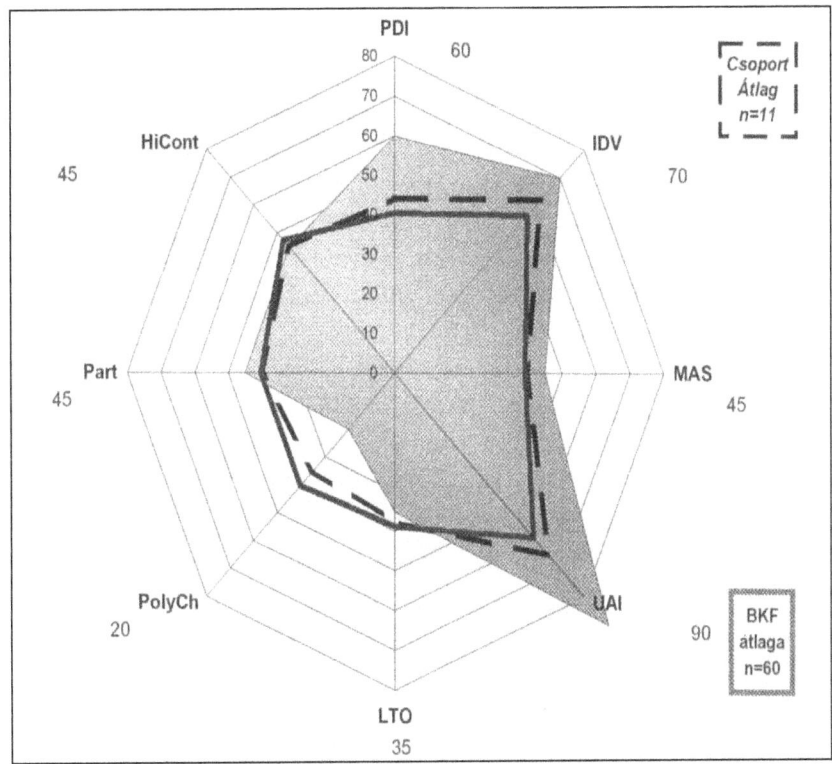

The continuous black line indicates the results obtained from questionnaires completed by the students of the Budapest University of Communication and Business, the broken line the average of the surveyed group, whereas the grey patch refers to Hofstede's (1983) original findings. These figures were constructed to illustrate the deviations in the case of each of Hofstede's (1983) dimensions. The figure explicitly illustrates the changes that took place over the past four decades.

4. Results

The following section of the paper will present only the dimensions where differences were perceived between the Hofstede (1983) and the Scope (2017) survey findings.

Our findings indicated that power distance results were 46 in the original Hofstede (1983) results, and the Scope (2017) findings showed 44, i.e. slightly lower scores. It means that hierarchy is retained by Hungarians for convenience only, and that it has become slightly, but still only slightly, less relevant for people. It also implies that superiors have become more accessible, control is disliked, and communication has become a bit more direct and participative.

Collectivism versus individualism scored 80 points in the 1970s, by now it has dropped to 60 points according to the recent Scope (2017) findings. In other words, Hofstede (1983) found that Hungarians were massively individualistic; our social network was loosely-knit and working relations were mostly contract-based. The new results refer to development in this dimension: Hungarians seem to have become more closely knit, they place greater emphasis on common than individual interest, and working relations have become necessary from the individual perspective (friendship, self-realisation) as well.

Femininity versus masculinity scores for Hungary were 88, and now this figure seems to be merely 40 points, a massive decrease (Scope, 2017). This plunge reveals that Hungarians are much less driven by competition, achievement, and success, equality between men and women is evolving, young husbands tend to share household and childcare chores, and women fulfil leader positions.

Hungarian uncertainty avoidance scored 82 four decades ago, and it now it has reduced to 58 according to Scope (2017) results. It indicates that Hungarians' preferences to avoid uncertainty seems to have vanished; they tend to embrace new global challenges and opportunities (e.g. working abroad and participation in dual degree programmes). However, they still need rules, but not orders imposed on them, as they are eager to work precisely and punctually.

The final dimension, long- versus short-term orientation, shows a similarly substantial fall from 58 to 41. It suggests that their link with the past, which used to be extremely strong due to historical reasons, have been softened by now. Instead of being pessimistic about our past, we focus on the present and plan for the future. We transform our traditions quickly to adjust to the present conditions, but they still have the propensity to save and invest.

5. Conclusions

In summary, the paper argued that teaching intercultural competencies for university students is one of the crucial goals at the Institute of Economic Technical Languages and Communication, Debrecen University. We emphasise the significance of students gaining a better understanding of their own cultural identity to be able to develop intercultural skills. The paper presented a new survey on changes in Hungarian culture.

Set against Hofstede's original findings in 1967-1973, the survey results by Scope (2017) suggest the following; due to historical reasons, adaptability and receptiveness have always been typical of Hungarians, and awareness of these skills is growing among the population as there is a recognition that this is the key to survival and progress (Kósa, 1999). The propensity to change in Hungarian people has also become a driver since Hofstede (1983) first carried out his survey. Finally, the inner strength of the nation to renew itself is not a new phenomenon: it could be observed in challenging moments in history and can be traced back to several centuries, for example during the invasion by the Ottomans, Habsburgs, and Soviets (Molnár, 2001).

Chapter 7

In developing the curriculum for the classes, our main aim is to foster the inclusion of improving intercultural skills in language teaching and the demonstration of intercultural competencies in classroom settings. If students lack the ability to perceive difference and similarity between their own culture and other cultures, they will not be able to develop intercultural competencies. Consequently, educators at the Institute of Economic Technical Languages and Communication provide trainings and lectures in the following topics to develop and enhance their intercultural skills: change management, emotional control, the study of facial expressions – based on research by Ekman and Friesen (2003) – and assertivity.

References

Altaf, A. (2011). The impact of organizational culture on organizational effectiveness: implication of Hofstede cultural model as organizational effectiveness model. *International Journal of Interdisciplinary Social Sciences*, 6(1), 161-174. https://doi.org/10.18848/1833-1882/CGP/v06i01/51996

Bakir, A., Blodgett, J. G., Vitell, S. J., & Rose, G. M. (2015). A preliminary investigation of the reliability and validity of Hofstede's cross cultural dimensions. In *Proceedings of the 2000 Academy of Marketing Science (AMS) Annual Conference* (pp. 226-232). Springer. https://doi.org/10.1007/978-3-319-11885-7_55

Beugelsdijk, S., Maseland, R., & Van Hoorn, A. (2015). Are scores on Hofstede's dimensions of national culture stable over time? A cohort analysis. *Global Strategy Journal*, 5(3), 223-240. https://doi.org/10.1002/gsj.1098

Brewer, P., & Venaik, S. (2011). Individualism–collectivism in Hofstede and GLOBE. *Journal of International Business Studies*, 42(3), 436-445. https://doi.org/10.1057/jibs.2010.62

Brewer, P., & Venaik, S. (2012). On the misuse of national culture dimensions. *International Marketing Review*, 29(6), 673-683. https://doi.org/10.1108/02651331211277991

Corey, C. M., Fok, L. Y., & Payne, D. M. (2014). Cross-cultural differences in values and conflict management: a comparison of us and Puerto Rico. *Journal Of Organizational Culture, Communications & Conflict*, 18(2), 59-78.

De Mooij, M., & Hofstede, G. (2010). The Hofstede model: applications to global branding and advertising strategy and research. *International Journal of Advertising*, 29(1), 85-110. https://doi.org/10.2501/S026504870920104X

Ekman, P., & Friesen, W. V. (2003). *Unmasking the face: a guide to recognizing emotions from facial clues.* Ishk.

European Commission. (2017). *ESCO strategic framework European skills, competences, qualifications and occupations.* Europen Commission

Falkné Bánó, K. (2002). Hungary, a bridge between East and West: cultural aspects of joining the New Europe. *EU Working Papers, 5*(2), 58-69. http://publikaciotar.repozitorium.uni-bge.hu/249/1/tek_2002_06.pdf

Fantini, A., & Tirmizi, A. (2006). *Exploring and assessing intercultural competence.* World Learning Publications, letöltés. http://digitalcollections.sit.edu/worldlearning_publications/1

Hall, E. T., & Hall, M. R. (1990). *Understanding cultural differences: [Germans, French and Americans]* (Vol. 9). Intercultural press.

Henning, J. (2016). *How behavioural component of increased cultural intelligence affects task performance in international intercultural working groups.* Doctoral dissertation. University of Pretoria. https://repository.up.ac.za/bitstream/handle/2263/59839/Henning_Behavioural_2017.pdf?sequence=1&isAllowed=y

Hofstede, G. (1980). Culture and organizations. *International Studies of Management & Organization, 10*(4), 15-41. http://dx.doi.org/10.1080/00208825.1980.11656300

Hofstede, G. (1983). National cultures in four dimensions: a research-based theory of cultural differences among nations. *International Studies of Management & Organization, 13*(1-2), 46-74. https://doi.org/10.1080/00208825.1983.11656358

Hofstede, G. (2006). What did GLOBE really measure? Researchers' minds versus respondents' minds. *Journal of international business studies, 37*(6), 882-896. https://doi.org/10.1057/palgrave.jibs.8400233

Hofstede, G. (2010). The GLOBE debate: back to relevance. *Journal of International Business Studies, 41*(8), 1339-1346. https://doi.org/10.1057/jibs.2010.31

Hofstede, G. (2011). Dimensionalizing cultures: the Hofstede model in context. *Online readings in psychology and culture, 2*(1), 1-26. https://doi.org/10.9707/2307-0919.1014

Hofstede, G. J. (2015). Culture's causes: the next challenge. *Cross Cultural Management, 22*(4), 545-569. https://doi.org/10.1108/CCM-03-2015-0040

Hofstede G, Hofstede, G. J., & Minkov, M. (2010). *Cultures and organizations: software of the mind* (3rd ed.). McGraw Hill.

Hofstede, G., & Minkov, M. (2010). Long-versus short-term orientation: new perspectives. *Asia Pacific business review, 16*(4), 493-504. https://doi.org/10.1080/13602381003637609

Hofstede, G., Neuijen, B., Ohayv, D. D., & Sanders, G. (1990). Measuring organizational cultures: a qualitative and quantitative study across twenty cases. *Administrative science quarterly, 35*(2), 286-316. https://doi.org/10.2307/2393392

Kieser, A. (1994). Book reviews: Geert Hofstede: cultures and organizations. Software of the mind: 1991, Maidenhead, UK: McGraw-Hill. 279 pages. *Organization Studies, 15*(3), 457-460. https://doi.org/10.1177/017084069401500308

Koops, L., Coman, L., Bosch-Rekveldt, M., Hertogh, M., & Bakker, H. (2015). Public perspectives on project success–influenced by national culture?. *Procedia-Social and Behavioral Sciences, 194*, 115-124. https://doi.org/10.1016/j.sbspro.2015.06.126

Kósa, L. (Ed.). (1999). *A cultural history of Hungary*. Corvina Books.

Lázár, T. (2017). Some sources of misunderstandings in intercultural business communication. *International Journal of Engineering and Management Sciences, 2*(3), 91-101. https://doi.org/10.21791/IJEMS.2017.3.9.

Molnár, M. (2001). *A concise history of Hungary*. Cambridge University Press.

Scope. (2017). *Budapest Intercultural Sensitivity Survey*. Intercultural Communication Services LLC.

Smith, P. B., Dugan, S., & Trompenaars, F. (1996). National culture and the values of organizational employees: a dimensional analysis across 43 nations. *Journal of cross-cultural psychology, 27*(2), 231-264.

Van Oudenhoven, J. P. (2001). Do organizations reflect national cultures? A 10-nation study. *International Journal of Intercultural Relations, 25*(1), 89-107. https://doi.org/10.1016/S0147-1767(00)00044-4

8 Intercultural competence in the language classroom

Marilena Minoia[1]

Abstract

The globalised world in which we live demands multilingual and cross-culturally aware professionals. The role of intercultural awareness is now, more than ever, crucial in the language classroom in order to allow students to become competent and independent adults who will be highly employable beyond graduation. The recently published Companion Volume (Council of Europe, 2018) of the Common European Framework of Reference (CEFR) points out the impact of interculturality on the learner by saying that "the learner does not simply acquire two distinct, unrelated ways of acting and communicating. The language learner becomes plurilingual and develops interculturality. The linguistic and cultural competences in respect of each language are modified by knowledge of the other and contribute to intercultural awareness, skills and know-how" (Council of Europe, 2001, p. 43). This paper reflects on the notion of interculturality and gives an overview of the methods used in a class of students from China to foster intercultural awareness. The range of activities implemented, the students' view on the practice and limitations of the project will also be presented.

Keywords: intercultural competence, professional competencies, Ningbo China Campus University of Nottingham, CEFR, language learning, higher education.

---

1. University of Nottingham, Nottingham, England; marilena.minoia@nottingham.ac.uk

How to cite this chapter: Minoia, M. (2019). Intercultural competence in the language classroom. In C. Goria, L. Guetta, N. Hughes, S. Reisenleutner & O. Speicher (Eds), *Professional competencies in language learning and teaching* (pp. 89-98). Research-publishing.net. https://doi.org/10.14705/rpnet.2019.34.917

Chapter 8

1. Introduction

Statistics published in April 2018 by the UK Council for International Student Affairs (www.ukcisa.org.uk) showed that 81% of students studying in higher education in the UK are from the UK, 6% are from the European Union (EU), and 13% are from the rest of the world. Amongst the latter, the number of Chinese students far exceeds any other nationality; almost one third of non-EU students in the UK are from China, the only country showing a significant increase in student numbers; a 14% rise since 2012-2013. The University of Nottingham contributes to this scenario with an established exchange programme in general, and with our overseas campuses in particular: with the opening of its campus in Malaysia in 2000, the University of Nottingham was the first UK university to open a branch campus overseas. This was then followed in 2004 by the opening of a campus in Ningbo, China. Students at the University of Nottingham in China or Malaysia can apply to study in Nottingham for a semester or a year through the Inter-Campus Exchange programme.

Given the University of Nottingham's pluricultural identity and the impact globalisation is having on graduate employment patterns, it is crucial to integrate an emphasis on intercultural awareness and competencies into the curriculum.

Increasing competitiveness in the world economy, the compelling need for viable solutions to global challenges and connectivity offered by social media create challenges as well as opportunities for citizens, businesses, and organisations. The ability to create successful connections with other countries largely depends on whether global citizens possess the necessary intercultural skills to effectively and respectfully communicate in a business environment.

The aim of this study is to explore strategies that may be implemented in the language classroom in order to foster the acquisition of intercultural competence as a crucial 'soft skill' for our students, the professionals of the future. This is a reflective paper that addresses the strategies adopted in an Italian language class to promote and enhance intercultural competence.

The study stems from the challenges encountered in teaching Chinese students in a Western institution. In the past, many scholars have compared the Chinese and the Western education style, and traditionally, it has been argued that Chinese learners tend to rely on memorisation, rote learning, and repetition (Gao & Ting-Toomey, 1998; Watkins & Biggs, 2001). In contrast, in Western contexts, where problem solving and critical thinking skills are to the fore, students seem to be encouraged to adopt a more Socratic pattern where the knowledge is generated or co-constructed (Greenholtz, 2003; Pratt, 1992).

Learning styles aside, this study focusses on the differences between the cultural profile of language learners, in this case Chinese students, and the culture of the target language, in this case Italian. It looks at the broader issue of teaching interculturalism in the language classroom, taking into consideration the challenges set by time constraints during the course of the delivery of a language module.

The strategies proposed in this study have been used throughout the academic year and they were aimed at promoting a reflection on the concept of interculturality in the learners.

2. Intercultural competence: the theory

Spitzberg and Chagnon (2009) define intercultural competence as "the appropriate and effective management of interaction between people who, to some degree or another, represent different or divergent affective, cognitive, and behavioural orientations to the world" (p. 7).

In the realm of the current higher education scene, the need to focus on intercultural competence has been reiterated by many scholars in the last decades. Alred, Byram, and Fleming (2003) argue that one of the primary purposes of education is to promote "a sense of interculturality, an intercultural competence, which is fundamental to education, perhaps always has been so, but is all the more significant in the contemporary world" (p. 6).

These ideas are finding increasing meaning across higher education institutions with the acknowledgement that intercultural competence is not only important to work in a global context, but is also a valuable skill to have in order to operate in our multicultural local communities (Jones, 2013, p. 97). This requires teachers "to adopt an inclusive approach to [the] curriculum and pedagogy and to recognize and value the cultural insights [that] our students, [as well as] staff, can offer and which might otherwise be overlooked" (Jones, 2013, p. 97).

In order to accommodate the needs of the globalised world in higher education, Green (2012, p. 1) suggests ten drivers for the internationalisation of the curriculum evidencing the strengths enhanced by a practice focussed on interculturality:

- to prepare students for 'global citizenship',
- to prepare students for the global workforce,
- to enhance the quality of teaching and research,
- to strengthen institutional capacity,
- to enhance prestige and visibility,
- to generate revenue,
- to contribute to local or regional economic development,
- to contribute to knowledge production on global issues,
- to solve global problems, and
- to increase international understanding and promote peace.

There is a large volume of published work describing the role of intercultural competence in the language classroom. In particular, Deardorff (2006, pp. 166-241) proposes the following model to define intercultural competence:

- **Attitudes**: the importance of valuing others through attitudes such as respect, curiosity, discovery, and openness, intended as a willingness to go beyond one's comfort zone.

- **Knowledge**: the importance of understanding the world from other people's perspectives based on sociolinguistic awareness.

- **Skills**: the acquisition and processing of knowledge through the practice of observing, analysing, interpreting, and relating.

- **Internal outcomes**: "these are aspects that occur within the individual as a result of the acquired attitudes, knowledge and skills necessary for intercultural competence [... leading] to an internal outcome that consists of [acquired] adaptability and empathy [towards the listener]" (Guan, 2012, p. 40).

- **External outcomes**: "[t]he [summation] of the attitudes, knowledge and skills, as well as the internal outcomes, are demonstrated through the behaviour and communication of the individual, which become the visible outcomes of intercultural competence experienced by others" (Guan, 2012, p. 40).

3. Methodology

The students involved in the study are Chinese students on exchange from the University of Nottingham China campus; they are students of Italian at level A1-A2 of the CEFR taking part in the exchange programme for the full academic year (2017-2018). The study involved an exceptionally small number of students (four) all of which are female and 19 to 20 year olds. This study is a reflection on the activities implemented to engage the students in a process of self-reflection and discovery of the concept of interculturality. The strategies used in class draw on Deardorff's (2006) model with the attempt to raise awareness of the culture of the self, the culture of the other, and each other's perspectives. In particular, seven sets of activities were devised following Deardorff's (2006) model.

3.1. Set 1: reflect on their own culture

This set aims to work on the concept of *knowledge* in Deardorff's (2006) model as it focusses on reflection on issues of cultural self-awareness. The students were asked to produce a guidebook, poster, presentation, or webpage in Italian for prospective visitors to their own town, country, or region. The aim of this activity was not only to describe the famous sites and national heritages, but also and foremost, to advise the visitor on cultural differences that could be encountered. As an example, the students chose to present on how to master using chopsticks in socially appropriate ways.

3.2. Set 2: become aware of how their culture is seen from another perspective

To foster critical thinking as a *skill* from Deardorff's (2006) model, the students were provided with a choice of articles and extracts from books, magazines, and websites in the target language and written by people who visited China. As an example, the students were provided with a few paragraphs from the book 'La Porta Proibita' by Tiziano Terzani (1985), an Italian journalist who reported from China for many years. Given the year of publication of the book, this also stirred discussions on changes that have taken place in China in the last 30 years.

3.3. Set 3: familiarise with sources of information about the target culture

Building on the Deardorff's (2006) concept of developing *attitudes* of curiosity and discovery, the students were exposed to films, news, podcasts, TV programmes, books, and magazines in the target language. During the course of the year, the students were regularly asked to discuss the content of something they had enjoyed reading or watching throughout the year.

3.4. Set 4: evaluating, observing and comparing skills; a travel photo diary on WhatsApp

This set of activities was based on the exploration of cultural clues and meanings, analysing and comparing results as *skills* towards the acquisition of intercultural competence (Deardorff, 2006). The students visited Italy during the Easter holidays. The trip was not part of the project, however, it seemed reasonable to exploit this opportunity in order to promote cultural reflections. The students were asked to take photos of things they considered culturally relevant and they were asked to comment and discuss them using WhatsApp as a common platform. For example, the students photographed little independent shops such as bakeries and patisseries, but also train stations, ticket machines, and bus timetables.

3.5. Set 5: increased exposure to Italian native speakers

To this end, an Italian student from the University of Nottingham was recruited as a volunteer to work on the project. She assisted the students with their classwork and she gave presentations on aspects of Italian culture such as the school system or going on holiday. She organised social events such as Italian cinema nights or outings with the Italian society. She acted as a valuable link to Italian culture at the university. The students benefited from the presence of this Italian student because they had the chance to be exposed to another Italian speaker who was not an academic. In line with Deardorff's (2006) model, this allowed for:

- enhanced listening skills (the student spoke particularly fast as she was not accustomed to slowing down the pace for pedagogical purposes);

- evaluating and comparing skills (comparing student lifestyles at the university); and

- an attitude of discovery and curiosity (students showed particular interest in the Italian students' lifestyles).

3.6. Set 6: critical thinking and self-reflection

Towards the end of the academic year, the students were asked to take part in video interviews in order to reflect on their internal outcomes (Deardorff, 2006). The students reflected on their experience of learning Italian in a British institution, the challenges, and what they had learned in the UK. All the students commented on their improved cultural awareness, and they showed a level of self-reflection that was extremely encouraging.

3.7. Set 7: the teacher's reflection and observation; a student survey

This activity allowed the teacher to observe the external outcomes (Deardorff, 2006). The students completed a survey that comprised of two questions. To the question: *Do you think that learning Italian made you think critically about your own culture and cultural differences?* all the interviewees gave positive responses. The students reported that they enjoyed the production of presentations on the geography and customs of their region of origin as this activity allowed them to have a different perspective on their own culture.

To the question: *Do you think you know more about Italian culture now?* the response was also in this case very positive. The students suggested that they felt empowered by the knowledge they acquired on geography, art, and history through the sets of activities adopted. Some students appreciated the opportunity they had to think about the stereotypes they had about Italy and they were able to recognise the similarities between the Chinese and Italian cultures.

4. Outcome and concluding remarks

The aim of this study was to explore and reflect on a range of methods to foster intercultural competence in the classroom. The results of this study show that students appreciated the activities proposed. In particular, they benefited from the reflective nature of the practice as they were able to consider their pre-conceptions and enjoyed engaging in a lasting process of learning on interculturality.

A number of limitations need to be considered in this particular study. Firstly, the small number of students involved in the project. This is a limitation in terms of the quantitative aspect of the research. More positively, due to time constraints during the academic year, it can often be challenging to explore different methods of delivery and teaching strategies. The small number of students involved in the project greatly facilitated this. Secondly, the study has only covered one academic year, and due to the qualitative nature of the research, it is difficult to verify if the results would have been as positive with another or larger group of students.

Although the current study is based on a small sample of participants, the findings provide evidence from the students' perspectives of the benefits of embedding practice that focusses on intercultural competence in the language class. This is evidenced in participant feedback where it is clear that they valued the exposure to the seven sets of culture-based activities proposed here.

Given the project's positive results, efforts will be made to extend this practice across the university's international campuses. It will also inform future research on the impact of intercultural competence-oriented methods in language teaching and learning.

The acquisition of intercultural competence does not happen over the course of one academic year. It is a lifelong process that requires further investigation in teaching and learning. The adoption of reflective practice may be a suitable method to work in the direction of intercultural competence acquisition.

References

Alred, G., Byram, M., & Fleming, M. (2003). *Intercultural experience and education.* Multilingual Matters.

Council of Europe. (2001). *Common European framework of reference for languages: learning, teaching, assessment.* Cambridge University Press.

Council of Europe. (2018). *Common European framework of reference for languages: learning, teaching, assessment. Companion volume with new descriptors.* https://rm.coe.int/cefr-companion-volume-with-new-descriptors-2018/1680787989

Deardorff, D. K. (2006). Identification and assessment of intercultural competence as a student outcome of internationalization. *Journal of Studies in International Education, 10*(3), 241-266. https://doi.org/10.1177/1028315306287002

Gao, G., & Ting-Toomey, S. (1998). *Communicating effectively with the Chinese.* Sage Publications. https://doi.org/10.4135/9781452220659

Green, M. F. (2012, April 15). *Universities must be clear and honest about internationalization.* University World News.

Greenholtz, J. (2003). Socratic teachers and Confucian learners: examining the benefits and pitfalls of a year abroad. *Language and Intercultural Communication, 3*(2), 122-130. https://doi.org/10.1080/14708470308668096

Guan, E. (2012). *Teach Chinese from cultural roots to local school culture: developing the Chinese teacher's and Australian students' intercultural competence.* Master's thesis. University of Western Sydney. http://researchdirect.uws.edu.au/islandora/object/uws%3A32233/datastream/PDF/download/citation.pdf

Jones, E. (2013). Internationalization and employability: the role of intercultural experiences in the development of transferable skills. *Public Money & Management, 33*(2), 95-104. https://doi.org/10.1080/09540962.2013.763416

Pratt, D. D. (1992). Chinese conceptions of learning and teaching: a Westerner's attempt at understanding. *International Journal of Lifelong Education, 11*(4), 301-319. https://doi.org/10.1080/0260137920110404

Spitzberg, B. H., & Chagnon, G. (2009). Conceptualizing intercultural competence. In D. K. Deardorff (Ed.), *The SAGE handbook of intercultural competence* (pp. 2-52). Sage.

Terzani, T. (1985). *La Porta Proibita.* Longanesi.

Watkins, D., & Biggs, J. (2001). *Teaching the Chinese learner: psychological and pedagogical perspectives.* The University of Michigan, Comparative Education Research Centre.

9. Embedding employability in language learning: video CV in Spanish

Chelo de Andrés[1]

Abstract

The drive to embed employability in Higher Education (HE) offers a growth opportunity for languages provision. The employability potential of language learning for the global graduate has been analysed by the *Born Global* project on languages and employability (British Academy, 2016). Employers have consistently identified communication and resilience, skills often imparted in learning language programmes, as highly sought after skills (World Economic Forum, 2018). Extensive evidence of the skill-set associated with language learning recently collected in the comprehensive volume *Employability for languages: a handbook*, edited by Corradini, Borthwick, and Gallagher-Brett (2016). In the same spirit of disseminating projects that equip students for real-life situations and introduce them to the world of work, this paper proposes the creation of a video CV as an innovative activity to integrate language learning and employability. Although the case study relates to Spanish, the process and steps identified can be easily adapted to other languages.

Keywords: employability, Spanish, language skills, global graduates, video CV, curriculum vitae.

---

1. University of Plymouth, Plymouth, England; chelo.andres@plymouth.ac.uk; https://orcid.org/0000-0003-1386-3633

How to cite this chapter: Andrés, C. de (2019). Embedding employability in language learning: video CV in Spanish. In C. Goria, L. Guetta, N. Hughes, S. Reisenleutner & O. Speicher (Eds), *Professional competencies in language learning and teaching* (pp. 99-109). Research-publishing.net. https://doi.org/10.14705/rpnet.2019.34.918

Chapter 9

1. Introduction

Embedding employability in the curriculum is a Higher Education Academy (HEA) driver that aims to align the needs of the business community, the country, and university students. Alongside this, Brexit challenges the UK's economy and its historical deficiency of language skills as reported by the British Council's (2017) *Languages for the future*. In this climate, language proficiency and the intercultural skills that it stimulates will increasingly become a sought after skill-set.

The *Languages and employability* section briefly discusses how this landscape affects language-teaching provision in HE and the opportunity afforded to make explicit their contribution to employability skills. Practitioners are developing innovative, creative, and work-related activities to embed employability. A case in point is the video CV activity discussed in the *Spanish for employability* section. Aside from the language and cultural awareness skills acquired, the activity fosters skills in the use of technology, reflective learning, collaboration, and resilience. Moreover, students learn how to present a positive and wholesome picture of self to prospective employers in Spanish, while gaining an understanding of how others see them, how to negotiate their own image in work environments, and how to collaborate with others.

The conclusion anticipated illustrates how embedding employability into language learning is at the heart of what language teaching professionals do. This truth needs to be made explicit when signposting students to the fact that what they learn in the language classroom translates into highly sought after skills in the world of work.

2. Languages and employability

The drivers for employability and their links to language provision are varied. Since 2010, prestigious bodies from the British Academy to the Confederation of British Industries (CBI) "are calling for a revival of languages to help maintain and improve UK research and business profiles in a global economy" (Andrés Martínez, 2011, p. 106). This call has become even more urgent nowadays with the UK government considering leaving the European Union.

In 2013, the HEA framework for employability espoused Knight and Yorke's (2003) assertion that employability is not just about employment, but "a set of achievements, skills, understanding and personal attributes that make graduates more likely to gain employment and be successful in their chosen occupations" (p. 2). Furthermore, the new parameters on Graduate Outcomes Records (GOR) will link to the Teaching Excellence Framework (TEF) from 2018 onwards. In other words, the post-graduation employability record of individual universities and departments will be under scrutiny not only for TEF classification but also for the promotion of programmes with excellent records of success in employability.

Almost a decade ago, the British Academy (2010) launched the *Language Matters* campaign to address an historical decline in Modern Foreign Languages (MFL) provision: "[t]he lack of language skills at secondary, tertiary and research levels will affect the UK's ability to compete effectively in a global market and to promote UK interests in a global context" (p. 1). More recently, the British Academy (2016) commissioned the *Born Global* research project; an up-to-date illustration of what the business landscape in relation to languages looks like. The project draws on data from a diversity of stakeholders such as professionals, executives, and small and medium-sized enterprises. Among the skills particularly appreciated by employers, it identifies a global mind-set and resilience, as well as analytical, linguistic, and intercultural awareness.

The CBI (2017) survey draws similar conclusions by identifying international cultural awareness; business and customer awareness skills as the weaknesses among graduate job seekers. Furthermore, it indicated that a third of employers were dissatisfied with graduates' attitudes and behaviours of self-management and resilience.

In this respect, Bernardette Holmes (2017), *Born Global* principal investigator, concludes that "the place of Britain on the world stage is likely only to diminish if its actors are restricted by their inability to communicate in any other language apart from English" (p. 4). Holmes (2017) urges language practitioners to make languages employability skills more visible. Against the background discussed so far, her call conveys a new sense of urgency.

There is also a call from political quarters to take on the *Born Global* recommendations. One such group is the All-Party Parliamentary Group (APPG) on Modern Languages, led by Baroness Cousins. The APPG called on all political parties for a commitment to promoting language learning in their 2015 manifesto (APPG, 2015). They stated that government figures show a loss of circa 50 billion GBP a year because of a deficiency of language skills in the workforce (Richardson, 2014). As mentioned by the British Academy (2014), "[t]he APPG argued that [...] better foreign language skills [were needed] not just for advancing individuals' education and skills, but to ensure [UK] economy, international engagement, defence, security and community relations remain competitive and sustainable" (para. 2). Holmes (2017) further states that "[t]he Brexit process [has] intensified the urgency to develop a multi-lateral [...] plan in education (from primary school to post-graduate research, including apprenticeships)" (p. 4). They call for specific actions to safeguard the UK's future requirements as a front-runner in the new global trade scenario and for assurances that the UK education system will produce sufficient linguists to meet its global needs on the international stage. These political allies' demands echo the call to make language study compulsory in primary and secondary education identified by *Born Global* (British Academy, 2016).

Likewise, the CBI has consistently stated that language skills are in shortage. Their 2009 survey indicated that only 27% of businesses did not need MFL skills to operate (CBI, 2009). This corroborates findings by the British Council (2011) survey where speaking another language was considered very or fairly important by 40% of employers. Last year's CBI survey exposed that just a third (34%) of businesses are satisfied with the foreign language skills of young people entering the job market (CBI, 2018). Their data also shows that employer satisfaction with the foreign language skills of those leaving education has declined sharply in the past year. It now stands at 34% compared to 42% in 2016. The report highlights the need for more and better language skills if Britain is to be successful as a global economy.

Despite powerful drivers to embed languages as employability skills in the HE curriculum and stakeholders calling for urgent solutions, serious concerns persist about how the UK is going to bridge the historical gap.

The next section proposes an intervention to respond to this call by making language students aware that they are learning highly sought after skills.

3. Spanish for employability: video CV

The creation of a video CV as an innovative project integrates language learning and employability. Equally, it equips students for real-life situations and introduces them to the world of work. Although the case study relates to Spanish, the process can be easily adapted to other languages. This project caters for students with B1 or near B1 level of the Common European Frame of Reference for languages (CEFR) of Spanish.

A close reference for our work here is the Corradini et al. (2016) volume. As per the activities proposed here, many of those contained in Section 3 of that volume aim to bring the workplace into the classroom. They not only involve students in the creation of their own content but also enable them to identify and articulate the specific personal and professional skills gained through classroom work.

Employability combines "personal qualities and beliefs, understandings, skillful practices and the ability to reflect productively on experience" (Owens & Tibby, 2014, p. 11). The creation of a video CV allows for the interplay and application of those factors. Activities undertaken during a six-week period as part of the project contribute to the creation of a formally assessed video CV. Additional informally assessed work-related activities such as writing a CV in Spanish and preparing for a job interview feed into the video's transcript.

Chapter 9

Following a three-fold process with clearly designed steps: *plan*, *record*, and *reflect*, students develop employment skills and self-awareness while practicing the language and learning about the labour market in Spain. The activities leading to the video CV encourage group work, interaction, effective communication, and reflection on experience. Step one, *plan*, concentrates on building vocabulary and identifying language related to the world of work in the Spanish job market. Step 2, *record*, focusses on drafting content, and writing work profiles and CVs using the vocabulary and expressions already acquired. In step 3, *reflect*, students compare the content they prepared in Step 2 and review a selection of published video CVs. This is the final stage prior to recording the individual video CVs for assessment. An account of each individual step follows below.

4. Description of the process for creating a video CV in Spanish

At the start of Semester 2, students learn that during six weeks they will be creating a video CV in Spanish. Students have access to computers to access online materials and databases for job information. Students like to talk about what work experience they have already had and about the area of work they would like to dedicate themselves after graduation. Each week, students complete a number of tasks culminating in the creation of a video CV.

4.1. Step one: plan

The project starts with warming up exercises where students build vocabulary by talking about professions and the skill-sets associated with them. Prompted by pictures of firefighters, carers, business entrepreneurs and such, students research the skills needed for each occupation. Next, they move to the personal dimension and talk about their work motivation before researching the Spanish job market for suitable employment via websites such as www.infojobs.net or infoempleo.com. They familiarise themselves with the description of job requirements and ideal candidate profiles for their ideal job. While practising their research skills, they utilise digital dictionaries and other resources such as www.wordreference.com, www.linguee.com, and translate.google.com, hence using digital and Information Communication Technology (ICT) skills.

In other words, when students are engaging in this first step, they are becoming self-aware of both what they can offer to the world of work and what the world of work has to offer them. They learn vocabulary related to the labour market, explore job market sites in a foreign language, and reflect on their personal goals and future ambitions.

4.2. Step two: record

During two weeks, students are often reminded that careful scripting, redrafting, and rehearsal are the key to a successful video CV. Students manage a variety of foreign language sources to create their work profile and reflect on the weakness and strengths of their own skill-set and personal qualities. To structure and create the first draft of paragraphs describing their qualifications, experiences, and personal qualities, the project follows a comprehensive unit on job hunting hosted by *Didactired*, a peer-reviewed repository of teacher resources, that is a sub-section of the Centro Virtual Cervantes (an organisation similar to the British Council). The unit, published in 2006 by Amparo Massó Porcar in collaboration with Maximiliano Alcañiz García, was based on a trade union document for migrant jobseekers (Massó Porcar & Alcañiz García, 2006; UGT, 2002). Students also explore CV digital templates available at Europass: https://europass.cedefop.europa.eu/documents/curriculum-vitae.

The group work feedback is a rewarding task where students read their personal profiles and welcome observations from peers. The efforts to negotiate meaning and consider whether the statements are too short and lacking in detail or too complex and need simpler utterances are very beneficial to all. Before implementing this task, students have already agreed to learn from each other and maintain an open mind to criticism of their work. One of the mantras they will hear is that 'we learn from our mistakes, and we learn from others' mistakes'. A relaxed atmosphere that allows for errors and failure while encouraging redrafting, rehearsal, and trying again is a strong strategy to build resilience.

During this step, students ask themselves how will the world receive what I have to offer. To develop higher levels of self-efficacy, self-confidence, and self-esteem, students must learn to reflect on and articulate their achievements (Halfpenny, 2016). Students are encouraged to do exactly that, they learn expressions to describe their qualities, they refine the vocabulary about essential and desirable skills, and learn how to present their weaknesses and strengths in a positive way to an employer.

4.3.   Step three: reflect

Before production of the video CV, the group watch selected video CVs and then evaluate them via discussion to identify the strengths and weaknesses. The videos themselves contain tips and reflections on what makes a good or bad video CV. According to Sas (2016), an advocate of video CV as a learning task, a video CV provides a "glimpse into who the candidate is like [as] person" (p. 2), better supporting interpersonal skills. Sas (2016) states that video CVs allow for enthusiasm and motivation to become visible, although it also poses risks such as inappropriate disclosure, poor performance, and unethical discrimination, which need to be discussed with students.

In this final stage, we follow Laura Alfonso's (2013) activity. Creating the video CV demonstrates perseverance and self-motivation. These are further skills that come to play as students redraft their content and take on cues and tips from the videos reviewed. Once again, students will rewrite to add sophistication to their scripts by including expressions to influence others or to express hope, uncertainty, etc. In Spanish, these language functions use the subjunctive mood, a challenge at B1 level. However, according to students, the 'real world' situation makes its practice less daunting.

Students have declined an extra session on editing videos with Microsoft Movie Maker, without the quality of the videos having suffered from it. The confidence and self-esteem students gain from making things is another life-long skill that can transfer to work related environments and boost students' employability prospects. Their video CVs tell their story so far under five, sometimes three minutes, and it is always a moment of gratification and wonder to see how much of the previous six weeks of work is actually evident in them.

5. Conclusion

Within the remit of the HEA framework for employability and similar drivers discussed in this paper, it is reasonable to conclude that the promotion of programmes with a strong reputation for employability will be considered more sustainable than those perceived as less successful to facilitate graduates' employment.

Against this background, it is important to emphasise the fact that language proficiency and the cultural awareness it develops could provide graduates with the career edge needed in a post-Brexit UK. As a highly sought after skill (39% of employers stated dissatisfaction with graduates' international cultural awareness), language's sustainability can be reinforced as a HE subject.

Language provision can bridge the gap and strengthen alliances with the political efforts of the APPG, the CBI, and the British Academy to fulfil UK future requirements as a front-runner in the new global and free trade scenario.

HE language teaching needs to make explicit its contribution to employability. Practitioners are developing innovative, creative, and flexible activities to embed employability in the curriculum. Such activities foster skills useful for developing emotional intelligence and intercultural skills, such as reflective learning, cultural awareness, and language skills.

According to students' feedback, this project helped them to retain vocabulary, improved their intonation and pronunciation, as well as teaching them strategies for interactions with interlocutors. Furthermore, they valued learning through assessment:

"I found this way of learning interesting and engaging";

"The activity was good and the assessment structure was suitable for engaging with learning".

Holmes (2017) advocates for a louder voice among language professionals to broadcast languages' added value. The author of this paper could not agree more with her statement.

References

Alfonso, L. (2013). No te quedes atrás. Haz tu vídeo CV. *RutaEle*. http://www.rutaele.es/wp-content/uploads/2013/07/R4_UD_No-te-quedes-atr%C3%A1s_Haz-tu-v%C3%ADdeo-CV_LAS_A2BC.pdf

Andrés Martínez, C. de (2011). Growing pains: a proposal to adopt aula virtual de Español (ave) for a blended learning beginners course. *Suplementos marcoELE, 13*, 105-111. http://marcoele.com/descargas/13/09.londres-andres.pdf?

APPG. (2015). *Manifesto for languages*. https://www.britishcouncil.org/sites/default/files/manifesto_for_languages.pdf

British Academy. (2010). *Language matters: a position paper*. https://www.thebritishacademy.ac.uk/sites/default/files/LanguageMatters2_0.pdf

British Academy. (2014). *British Academy welcomes manifesto for languages by all-party parliamentary group on modern languages*. https://www.thebritishacademy.ac.uk/news/british-academy-welcomes-manifesto-languages-all-party-parliamentary-group-modern-languages?

British Academy. (2016). *Born Global* project. http://www.britac.ac.uk/policy/Born_Global.cfm

British Council. (2011). *The global skills gap: preparing young people for the new global economy*. https://think-global.org.uk/wp-content/uploads/dea/documents/BusinessPoll_online_TG.pdf

British Council. (2017). *Languages for the future*. https://www.britishcouncil.org/organisation/policy-insight-research/languages-future-2017

CBI. (2009). *Future fit: preparing graduates for the world of work*. Universities UK. https://www.universitiesuk.ac.uk/policy-and-analysis/reports/Documents/2009/future-fit-preparing-graduates-for-the-world-of-work.PDF

CBI. (2017). *Helping the UK thrive: CBI/Pearson education and skills survey 2017*. Confederation of British Industry. http://www.cbi.org.uk/insight-and-analysis/helping-the-uk-thrive/

CBI. (2018). *Educating for the modern world, CBI/Pearson education and skills annual report*. Confederation of British Industry. http://www.cbi.org.uk/cbi-prod/assets/File/CBI%20Education%20and%20Skills%20Annual%20Report%202018.pdf

Corradini, E., Borthwick, K., & Gallagher-Brett, A. (Eds) (2016). *Employability for languages: a handbook*. Research-publishing.net. https://doi.org/10.14705/rpnet.2016.cbg2016.9781908416384

Halfpenny, S. (2016). *A practical model of graduate employability*. https://yorkforum.org/2016/06/03/a-practical-model-of-graduate-employability/

Holmes, B. (2017). *Global Britain requires more and better language skills*. https://www.repository.cam.ac.uk/bitstream/handle/1810/269992/Holmes.pdf?sequence=1

Knight, P., & Yorke, M. (2003). *Learning, curriculum and employability in higher education*. Routledge Falmer. https://doi.org/10.4324/9780203465271

Massó Porcar, A., & Alcañiz García, M. (2006). *Busco trabajo in Didactired, Centro Virtual Cervantes*. https://cvc.cervantes.es/aula/didactired/anteriores/mayo_06/01052006a.htm

Owens, J., & Tibby, M. (2014). *Enhancing employability through enterprise education: examples of good practice in higher education*. The Higher Education Academy. https://www.heacademy.ac.uk/system/files/resources/enhancing_employability_through_enterprise_education_good_practice_guide.pdf

Richardson, H. (2014, July 14). Modern languages 'recovery programme' urged by MPs. *BBC News*. https://www.bbc.com/news/education-28269496

Sas, C. (2016). *Technologies for employability*. HEA Conference Transforming teaching and learning in STEM, 28-29 January, Nottingham, UK. http://eprints.lancs.ac.uk/81873/1/Technologies_for_Employability_paper_final.pdf

UGT. (2002). *Manual de Técnicas de Búsqueda Activa de Empleo para Inmigrantes*. Union General de Trabajadores. http://www.redincola.org/download_fic.php?id=63

World Economic Forum. (2018). *Forum of jobs report*. http://www3.weforum.org/docs/WEF_Future_of_Jobs_2018.pdf

10. Sharing the Year Abroad experience with non-language students: a student-led project on outward mobility

Anna de Berg[1]

Abstract

Whilst internationalisation has already become an integral part of the curriculum at all higher education institutions in the UK, what does it actually mean? Is student mobility an aim in itself or is it more useful as a promotional tool to develop more internationally oriented graduates? How can we help students take control over their intercultural learning? This article analyses a recent student-led project undertaken by final-year Modern Foreign Languages (MFL) students at Sheffield Hallam University (SHU) to promote outward mobility among students on non-language degree programmes against the backdrop of current discussions surrounding internationalisation. It examines advantages, constraints, and drawbacks of such a project and presents some ideas for future consideration. The project has been developed and managed by the author of this article (module and project leader and Faculty International Mobility coordinator) in collaboration with the Head of International Partnerships at SHU.

Keywords: internationalisation, student experience, mobility, global engagement.

---

1. Sheffield Hallam University, Sheffield, England; a.deberg@shu.ac.uk

How to cite this chapter: De Berg, A. (2019). Sharing the Year Abroad experience with non-language students: a student-led project on outward mobility. In C. Goria, L. Guetta, N. Hughes, S. Reisenleutner & O. Speicher (Eds), *Professional competencies in language learning and teaching* (pp. 111-120). Research-publishing.net. https://doi.org/10.14705/rpnet.2019.34.919

1. Introduction

Discussions surrounding internationalisation of higher education, and most specifically its curricula, have been the subject of extensive research for over a decade now (Brewer & Cunningham, 2009; Deardorff & Arasaratnam-Smith, 2017; De Wit, 2011; Knight, 2009; Leask, 2009, 2015; Maringe & Foskett, 2012; Streitwieser, 2014; Williams & Lee, 2015). This article focusses on a practitioner's perspective and therefore does not include a more complex literature review; instead, it presents some ideas on embedding internationalisation in the curriculum and analyses the practicality of these in an institutional context. For the benefit of other practitioners, it outlines in detail the project (context and project description) and discusses its positive outcomes and drawbacks (evaluation), drawing attention to some discrepancies between the theory and practice, and making recommendations for consideration of senior management, MFL lecturers, tutors, and global mobility coordinators (recommendations and conclusion).

2. Context

Sheffield Business School at SHU is home to applied undergraduate dual language degree programmes with International Business, Marketing, or Tourism. Like in other UK institutions, language students spend a compulsory period abroad, but, unlike other universities, SHU students are required to spend 18 months abroad, studying and working in France, Germany, Italy, or Spain. After their return, most of the students will take a final-year consultancy module called Languages and Cultures in the Global Workplace (LCGW), which allows them to apply the linguistic and intercultural skills gained during their placements to a specific, real-life project for selected local or international companies and organisations. Traditionally, at least one project per year would be commissioned by SHU; in the past, this would involve projects aimed at improving the international student experience as well as collaborating with the language society on a series of integration events for home and exchange students. All projects are supported by Venture Matrix, an employability team that liaises between the university and external stakeholders, and provides professional advice to both employers and students.

3. Project description

In 2017/2018, the international SHU project was commissioned by the Head of International Partnerships for the Faculty of Business (Sheffield Business School) and was specifically designed to address first-year home students in an attempt to increase the outgoing student numbers in the faculty and promote outward mobility among students on non-language degree programmes. Also in 2017/2018, Venture Matrix entered a three-year long partnership with Santander Universities: every year, Santander will financially support a module which enables students to use their skills to collaborate with organisations abroad and further develop their employability skills. The first module to receive the financial help was the LCGW module. It was decided that the final-year students would plan and organise an 'Erasmus Taster Trip' to two European partner universities and invite along a group of first-year students with the aim of encouraging them to take part in the outward mobility the year after.

Eight final-year students on Languages with International Business, Marketing, and Tourism programmes were assigned to this project: they worked in two groups of four, developing marketing strategies and promoting study abroad opportunities in the faculty while also conducting market research and monitoring social media ('students-to-students') connected to mobility. Both groups delivered two complex group reports analysing perceived barriers to outward mobility as well as proposing feasible solutions to tackle the issue based on extensive market research. They also developed promotion strategies to increase the outgoing student numbers, e.g. among others, targeting prospective students at open days with talks and specially designed materials. The most attractive part of the projects were, however, the Erasmus trips: students organised them with the help of the partner institutions abroad – University of Applied Sciences in Amsterdam and Haaga-Helia University of Applied Sciences in Helsinki. They advertised the opportunity in the faculty and shortlisted ten first-year students after having read their expressions of interest. The main criteria for the selection, suggested by the Head of International Partnerships, was the applicants' international experience (or, rather, the lack thereof), their expectations from the trips (take away the fear of the unknown), and intellectual curiosity towards the other. At the end, the students conducted formal interviews and invited eight first-year students to join them on the trips.

Both partner universities welcomed the groups in January 2018 by organising extensive campus tours. In Helsinki, the group was also invited to take part in admissions interviews for international students: an opportunity that was extremely well received. Both groups also organised tailor-made workshops about intercultural communication and the Erasmus experience. After their return, the first-year students were asked to fill in feedback questionnaires indicating their level of satisfaction and measuring their (basic) intercultural awareness. The results and evaluation were very positive, however, only four out of eight students decided to apply for the mobility. One student admitted having social anxiety and not feeling comfortable spending a semester in a foreign environment, one decided to withdraw from the university for unrelated reasons, and two did not give any reason at all (see the next section for more detailed information).

The assessment in the module is 100% a portfolio: the students submitted a 3,000-word group report (one per group), two individual reflections, one on team and personal performance and another academic one on cultural awareness and its applicability in the project, as well as a number of individual research tasks, which all fed into the group report. The research findings were extremely valuable from the faculty's perspective, and some of the recommendations have already been implemented; the social media accounts are now also being populated with data by the student international officers in the language society.

If a similar project should be run in the future again, resources permitting, some amendments would have to be proposed to increase its effectiveness: an early information about the available funding, more focus on the first-year students' impressions (evaluation beyond standard questionnaires, potentially reflections or audio-visual presentations), and a long-reaching follow-up to allow the students to record their after-mobility reflections and evaluation of their experiences with a potential continuation beyond their graduation.

4. Evaluation of the project (trips)

The student project, although it included a well-designed and useful international experience and focussed on building awareness of study abroad opportunities, has not fulfilled its objectives entirely. It was an attempt to internationalise the faculty, but because of the short time frame and lack of suitable resources needed for a more thorough preparation, not all of the elements of the project were successful. In the following, I shall use the broad definition of the curriculum as it is used by Betty Leask (2015) in her *Internationalizing of the Curriculum*, where the term curriculum "includes all aspects of the learning/teaching situation" (Leask, 2015, p. 7, following Kemmis & Fitzclarence's 1991 definition) rather than just the list of topics of study. The curriculum is hence a blend of three interactive elements that all contribute to the student learning experience: the formal, the informal, and the hidden curriculum (certain decisions to include or exclude some content from the formal and informal curriculum).

While the project itself was part of the formal curriculum (students *must* work on a consultancy project in their final year), students were given certain freedom in designing the actual activities and engaging first-year students in a series of extra-curricular events. However, as previously explained, the project or, more precisely, the Erasmus Taster Trips, did not bring the expected outcomes: only 50% of the first-year students decided to go abroad as a result of this experience. While the reasons behind their decision might be prosaic, the question remains whether the project was developed with the right set of objectives and the right focus. Had the activities been prepared with a different angle or using more resources on campus before and after the visits abroad rather than on the actual trips, would more first-year students have decided on applying for an exchange afterwards?

The answer requires looking at the trips – or, by extension, outward mobility – as a means to create a shift in the mentality of the students, rather than an end product: increasing the number of students going abroad. This concept is not new in the discourse surrounding internationalisation of higher education (Brewer & Cunningham, 2009; Brewer & Leask, 2012; De Wit, 2011; Knight, 2009; Leask, 2015). Leask (2009) distinguishes between the process of internationalisation of the curriculum and the end product of the process, which is an internationalised curriculum. In creating the right conditions and developing an understanding of what internationalisation means, we devised an internationalised curriculum which "will engage students with internationally informed research and cultural and linguistic diversity and purposefully develop their international and intercultural perspectives as global professionals and citizens" (Leask, 2009, p. 209).

When analysing the results of the project, it becomes clear that the 'purposeful development' of both the first- and final-year students' intercultural perspectives did not receive enough attention in the preparation phase for the trips. There are several factors which played a significant role here: the module is a final-year module taken by students who just returned from their work placements abroad, hence had a one year break from studying and taking relevant modules; all projects were developed and approved shortly before the new academic year (as is common) and the allocation of projects was done randomly for the purpose of fairness and, finally, the information about the available funding came late, and therefore, the taster trips were added to the projects as an ad-hoc component, which was not planned in the initial phase. Therefore, the expectation that all first-year students would apply for the study exchange after their return from the taster trips and that all final-year language students will have experienced a boost in confidence as a result of the intercultural mentoring they have been asked to do, was simply unrealistic.

The 'purposeful development' rooted in the internationalised curriculum did not take place due to the factors mentioned above, but also due to the fact that international mobility is too often synonymous with intercultural competence (De Wit, 2011; Knight, 2009; Leask, 2015) – a common misconception that has influenced some of the project's learning outcomes. Instead of concentrating on the development of the right conditions and building on a deep understanding of processes of internationalisation, the project was focussed on one aim: to convince the non-specialist students to go abroad, without explaining in more detail why they should do it and why this was crucial for their own future.

It is also an acceptable conclusion that the final-year language students were equally unprepared from this perspective, although their own account of the trips and the feedback they received from the first-year students were overwhelmingly positive. They had the advantage of having gone through the experience of living abroad – most of them spent their study abroad semester in one country and worked in another for a full year – but after the return, they were not offered the possibility of a more meaningful reflective evaluation of their intercultural experience beyond the standard placement report with reflective elements, which was briefly discussed with their coordinators and tutors.

Therefore, the students, equipped with what they perceived as a wealth of international experience, became uncomfortably self-aware of the gaps created by the exclusivity of the knowledge of the 'specific country only' (i.e. France, Germany, Italy, Spain). In other words, the experience they relied upon exposed that they were not fully prepared to claim the 'global citizenship' they have been truly confident about, as they struggled (even if less so) with the same issues in Finland and the Netherlands as their younger peers – foreign language, food, and customs. This became particularly apparent in the oral evaluation of the trips that took place just after their return.

This task can also be seen as an example of a 'hidden message' of the (informal) curriculum: by requesting that the first-year students take part in a workshop and discuss the learning outcomes with them, but without making the effort to request to participate beforehand in a similar training themselves, the final-year students made assumptions about their own suitability as intercultural trainers and underestimated their own intercultural competence.

5. Recommendations and conclusion

The final-year language degree programme students were given a difficult task to handle: they had to convince a group of students without any linguistic background or intercultural awareness to apply for a study semester abroad. Given the already mentioned institutional constraints, there is no doubt that they acted professionally and responsibly and managed to create an inclusive environment for the first-year students, who indicated at the beginning of the project that they did not think about studying abroad in the future. Still, 50% of them will be studying abroad as a result of this experience.

How can projects like this one be better embedded in the curriculum, then? A change in mentality and attitudes at many levels is a *sine qua non* of a successful process of internationalisation of the curriculum. It requires attention and increased resources from various stakeholders: faculty deans, heads of departments, members of staff, administrative support, etc. (cf. Brewer & Leask, 2012), but it also requires a better understanding of what an internationalised curriculum means for the students. This gap between the theory, the expectations of the senior management, and the actual reality of the classroom means that the process of internationalisation is more of a challenge than perhaps expected.

The project on promoting outward mobility, although a truly important experience for the language degree programme students, is not enough to introduce the changes that would impact on the curriculum as such, and enthuse the development of 'global skills' in *all* students. It is important, however, because it demonstrates the capability of language students to reflect and share the reflection with non-language students for whom this experience might be truly transformational. Naturally, any complex changes in the curriculum can only be agreed formally as part of the institutional strategy, but I shall point out a few possible areas (adapted from Leask, 2015) where MFL lecturers and tutors could offer specific guidance based on their own expertise in area studies and intercultural communication.

First of all, we should encourage a positive transformation of the institutional internationalisation strategy to shift the focus in the curriculum from looking at the specific activity, which only addresses a small number of students, to concentrating on the content of the whole module/course, its learning outcomes, and assessment. This goes beyond the assessment criteria of a given module: in the internationalised curriculum, the students should also be regularly and consistently assessed on their progress in developing intercultural competence using a variety of specially designed assessment tools online (cf. Fantini, 2009). Secondly, the language classes – traditionally relatively small in numbers and hence offering the perfect setting for a personalised approach and time for intercultural preparation – could be the ideal place for learning to become truly transformative, i.e. causing a shift in mentality (cf. Brewer & Cunningham, 2009, using Mezirow's 1997 research), which can only happen when the students are ready to face new experiences and able to deal with the cognitive and emotional dissonance they will most likely be exposed to during a year abroad (Brewer & Cunningham, 2009). Finally, we should encourage our language students to act as ambassadors to promote the benefits of outward mobility and share their experience in formal and informal settings: through special events, organised societies, formal seminars in intercultural competence (both before and after the mobility), but also, like in the discussed project, as part of their ambassadors' role during open days – reaching out to prospective students early on, thus preparing a foundation for their possible future interest in international study or work placement opportunities. Only by designing an internationalisation strategy truly and consistently rooted in the curriculum can we help our students become global graduates.

Acknowledgements

The project was funded by Santander Universities and supported logistically by Venture Matrix (Sheffield Hallam University).

References

Brewer, E., & Cunningham, K. (Eds). (2009). *Integrating study abroad into the curriculum: theory and practice across the disciplines*. Stylus Publishing LLC.

Brewer, E., & Leask, B. (2012). Internationalization of the curriculum. In D. K. Deardorff, H. de Wit, J. D. Heyl & T. Adams (Eds.) *The SAGE handbook of international higher education* (pp. 245-265). Sage. https://doi.org/10.4135/9781452218397.n14

De Wit, H. (2011). Internationalization of higher education: nine misconceptions. *International Higher Education, 64,* 6-7.

Deardorff, D. K., & Arasaratnam-Smith, L. A. (Eds). (2017). *Intercultural competence in higher education.* Routledge.

Fantini, A. E. (2009). Assessing intercultural competence: issues and tools. In D. K. Deardorff (Ed.), *The SAGE handbook of intercultural competence* (pp. 456-476). Sage.

Kemmis, S., & Fitzclarence, L. (1991). *Curriculum theorising: beyond reproduction theory.* Deakin University.

Knight, J. (2009). Five myths about internationalization. *International Higher Education, 62,* 14-15.

Leask, B. (2009). Using formal and informal curricula to improve interactions between home and international students. *Journal of studies in international education, 13*(2), 205-221.

Leask, B. (2015). *Internationalizing the curriculum.* Routledge.

Maringe, F., & Foskett, N. (Eds). (2012). *Globalization and internationalisation in higher education.* Continuum.

Mezirow, J. (1997). Transformative learning: theory to practice. *New Directions for Adult and Continuing Education, 74,* 5-12.

Streitwieser, B. (Ed.). (2014). *Internationalisation of higher education and global mobility.* Symposium Books.

Williams, R. D., & Lee, A. (Eds). (2015). *Internationalizing higher education.* Sense Publishers.

11. Can students be knowledge creators? A case study

Ruth Whittle[1]

Abstract

Enthused about Healey's (2017) concept of approaching student learning as a creative process in which students could be partners (see also Healey, Flit, & Harrington, 2016; Healey & Jenkins, 2009), I re-designed one of my existing courses to follow this approach. My case study explores how I introduced students to the concept, the methodology I used to define what research should look like on the course, and how I harnessed students' choices to minimise the potential risks involved for them as well as for myself as a teacher. This is followed by a report on student feedback as well as further reflections on how to redesign learning outcomes and align the assessment format to those outcomes.

Keywords: students as partners, students as knowledge creators, assessment of knowledge creation, alignment of learning outcomes and assessment.

1. Rationale

At conferences focussing on teaching and learning, it is easy to observe that academics tend to participate because they want to find out 'what's out there' in the pedagogy of their discipline; they may like to try new things or have had the kind of feedback from students that encourages them to explore a pedagogical approach which is new to them. Considering students as knowledge creators and therefore partners is quite extreme when it comes to risk-taking:

---

1. University of Birmingham, Birmingham, England; r.whittle@bham.ac.uk; https://orcid.org/0000-0003-3700-186X

How to cite this chapter: Whittle, R. (2019). Can students be knowledge creators? A case study. In C. Goria, L. Guetta, N. Hughes, S. Reisenleutner & O. Speicher (Eds), *Professional competencies in language learning and teaching* (pp. 121-131). Research-publishing.net. https://doi.org/10.14705/rpnet.2019.34.920

- Will the students be willing to be in the driving seat or be fearful or negative about this?

- Will the learning outcomes still be reached, i.e. will this course still be academically sound?

- Will the students' marks be what they expected, i.e. good, leading to a 2.1, at least?

- Will students take me seriously if I pass authority to them; might they see this as an abdication of my duties as 'their' lecturer?

- Will my 'approval rating' in the module evaluations be detrimental to my standing and career?

Following Healey's (2017) TED talk about the benefits of engaging students as 'partners in research and inquiry' at the 2017 University of Birmingham Teaching and Learning Conference, I considered that my final-year course in German studies, *Sex, Submission, and Seduction*, might be suitable for trying myself.

My aim was to get students away from surface learning, and to engage more deeply. I wanted to rouse their interest in research and considered the responsibility of being partners in research a characteristic that demonstrably aligned with my faculty's goal to equip our students "with the knowledge and skills they need to become independent problem-solvers and natural leaders" (College of Arts and Law, n.d., p. 5).

2. Introducing the students to being knowledge creators

In this 20-credit German module, with two hours of class time for 20 weeks on a Friday afternoon, students are expected to

> "gain a **historical perspective** on the **diversity** of women's writing in the period and on the key topics, be they **negotiated** directly or indirectly: the **place of 'woman'** in society, the relationship with 'man', and the role of relationships in defining one's **identity**" (Excerpt from module description).

In this case, the 'historical perspective' spanned texts from the 19th to the end of the 20th century, from pre-World War I (Bertha von Suttner, Lou-André Salomé, and Theodor Fontane) to post-Reunification (Judith Hermann) via Maxie Wander and Christa Wolf. The diversity of women protagonists in men's and women's writing spanned the topics of war, women and education in the bourgeois society or in a socialist society, women and work, and women within their family and in illicit relationships. How women negotiated their identity was to be explored in all of these texts, under those aspects, and through some secondary reading (both historical and sociological).

The course was to be relevant to students in more than one regard: at the end of the course, students should be able to reflect on their own – gendered – identity and relate this to other texts and contexts they would come into contact with – their future workplace, their friendships, their position in the family etc, beyond having something to say about the texts we read and grasping the historical perspective.

The first task, however, was for the students to understand what to expect:

- they could be researchers but there should be nothing to fear;

- research usually did not present one valid answer only, and thus ambiguity had to be embraced;

- being co-creators would entail them taking responsibility for finding answers; this could actually be enjoyable; and

- choices would need to be made by them, not by their teachers.

Following Brew's (2012, p. 102) advice that the notions of 'research' and 'scholarship' need to be clear before one can operate with them in the classroom, I used a technique which I had gleaned from Katarina Mårtensson at a keynote she gave at the EuroSoTL Conference (University of Lund, June 2017). Instead of giving some definitions of 'research', I used images in order to demonstrate research in action: I had taken a number of photos of an art installation at the Charlottenburg Palace Art Gallery in Copenhagen, along one of the most famous harbour quays (Nyhavn) in the world.

Initially, I showed a picture of the installation taken from a distance and asked what the students thought the windows were made of but did not mention the purpose of the building to them (Figure 1).

Figure 1. Charlottenburg Palace Art Gallery, from a distance

The students discussed possible answers with each other and with me. Everyone was happy to provide a suggestion. I then showed the installation from close up, i.e. a part of a window (Figure 2).

It was now clear that the colours which students had seen and which had led their suggestions were of life vests.

Figure 2. Charlottenburg Palace Art Gallery, close-up

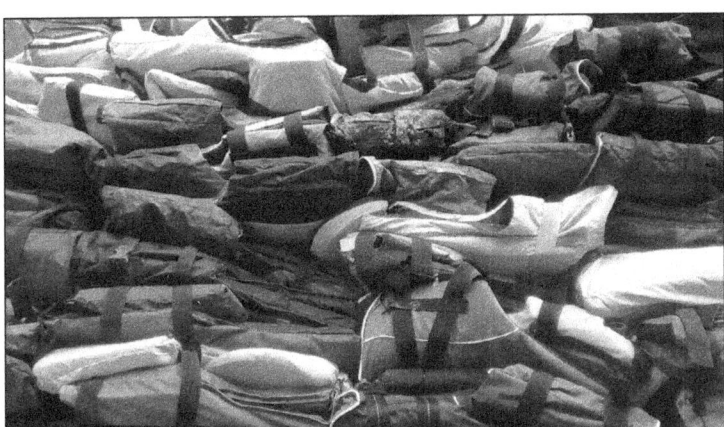

After students had expressed their surprise and come to terms with what these objects in the windows actually were, I explained how the process we had just gone through mirrored research.

Research is an iterative process: looking from afar, looking up close, trying out different perspectives, and being aware of one's chosen perspective. However, it's not just about recognising life vests, but it's also about what they might mean to the viewers in the particular context in which they find them: in seafaring Copenhagen, life vests may be an everyday occurrence to many, but that is not the case for a viewer from, say, Birmingham. However, the connection to water is made explicit through the location of the museum along the quays. At the same time, media reports in the summer of 2017, when I had taken the pictures, were replete with images of refugees who had arrived on the Isle of Lesbos in Greece or had been picked up by rescue boats on the Mediterranean. For the inhabitants of Lesbos, the life vests which refugees had abandoned once they were on shore were rubbish, for the refugees on boats in the Mediterranean they might or might not provide safety if they fell into the water (Ecojesuit, 2016). Everyone in the group has their own personal thoughts on the European refugee crisis, some may not ever have been verbally expressed, but my group of students immersed themselves in this exercise and gained some confidence in the fact that we were all equally able participants.

By exchanging first impressions and trying to locate where they came from, students experienced how first impressions may need to be revised, that they are not simply objectively verifiable but can be interpreted differently when set in or associated with different contexts. Currently, a search on Google Images for 'discarded life jackets on Lesbos' brings up dozens of photos, from all perspectives, of piles of life jackets in exactly the colour mix which the windows in Copenhagen display, making the idea that research is an iterative process even more tangible. Students were also asked to evaluate their responses: different qualities are valid, not just rational ones but also feelings; however, you need to relate your feelings to the object you perceive convincingly.

Having made sure that students had grasped this concept of research, I confronted them with the challenge: would they want to be researchers in the way I had just demonstrated or did they want to be at the receiving end of 'teaching'? In order to help students conceptualise the choice, I showed them Jenkins and Healey's (2005) early diagram on "the role of the teacher and the students" (p. 22).

I ascertained that they were able to relate the diagram to what we had just discussed about research and then asked them to discuss, among themselves, where on the respective axes they wanted to be, and therefore wanted me to be. I left the room for a few minutes, until they were ready to let me know their choice. They told me that they had chosen to be knowledge creators as that was something that nobody had entrusted them with so far, and they were curious to try it out. At this early stage, students showed a promising level of enterprise. However, it is important then to continue with the challenge and require students to make some choices then and there.

3. Choices to make

Students needed to discuss, among themselves, first on how they would like this course to be shaped. It is unrealistic to shape it from scratch at the beginning of the academic year. The course intranet site was already populated with a skeleton structure, there were some set texts, and what I considered a reasonable amount of time for them, there was a resource list and a discussion board for anyone in the group to post any other sources on our topics which we wanted to share.

Bearing this in mind, students decided that it was difficult to decide on shape straight away. The following suggestions were agreed upon, and subsequently put on the course intranet site for all to refer to during the course.

- Sessions should include presentations on secondary literature; five minutes or more at the beginning of each session, then a discussion to set focus; this demands reading.

- Students want to see where discussions were going in each session; plan next session at end of each session.

- Where there is a choice, they want to read fewer rather than more texts, and have a more detailed discussion and secondary reading.

Following this outline, students were asked to think about the challenges of the course, again without me, the teacher, in the room. After a few minutes, when I was asked to return to the room, it was interesting that they had already started to think about solutions, and during their report to me, included those.

Students realised that they may have different views on which topic or text to concentrate on next. They decided that they would let me, the lecturer, know on a Monday morning, once the class had discussed among themselves (mostly via their Whatsapp group). The group included native speakers of English as well as of German (Erasmus students), and the group decided that we would have discussions in both German and English to benefit both Erasmus and home students. There were no concerns that anyone would be left behind through choice of one or the other language. Students expected their responsibility as co-creators to bring with it a lot of work and pressure, but also the opportunity for them to develop an interest and their language. This, they thought, would allow them to develop ownership and make taking exams 'normal'. Furthermore, students observed that they were usually tired on a Friday afternoon, but suggested a coffee and cake break; a loose rota was drawn up, where the responsibility for contributing coffee, tea, a kettle, milk, and edibles were shared out among all, and this relying on others proved justified throughout the year.

Additionally, I was keen to establish ground rules which would limit the risks outlined at the start of this paper. Based on the experience which the group, including the teacher, had of discussions to this point, it was determined that mutual respect would be required, that students/staff needed to talk openly among and to each other and bring to the fore anything that was not going right as well as suggest solutions.

4. Feedback

In informal feedback in class at the end of Semester 1, students thought that the first long text had not been ideal but also considered that that reading experience had given them more appreciation for the other 19th-century texts. As I do not entirely want to lose the topic of that text, 'war and women', I have replaced it with one political treatise (Dohm, 1917: 'Der Missbrauch des Todes') and one short story (Suttner, 2005/1897): 'Gott verzeihe ihr') in 2018/2019.

In order to get more buy-in and less push-back to texts read in class in my modules, I have, on several occasions, sent excerpts of texts I proposed to participants during the summer break and invited them to choose and comment on the reasons for their choice. Whilst students were aware that they had had a choice and comments such as 'too much reading' subsequently disappeared completely from student feedback despite them not reading less than before, I have always had very few responses to my invitation to choose, so basing what is being read on those choices did not bring the additional buy-in that I had hoped for nor could it be considered inclusive or democratic.

Students' formal feedback at the end of the course via the institutional online module evaluation questionnaire was very encouraging. They did indeed consider the course a joint endeavour and in the 'what could be done differently' section suggested some more guidance might be needed, but this was not specified further. Students were invested in the course and also acknowledged the lecturer's investment. They commented that the course had been inclusive, nobody felt left behind for reasons of language, background, subject combination, or disability. In my view, the feedback could not have been more positive or constructive. The risk of the teacher losing authority or appearing distant did not materialise. To the contrary: rather than being commented on (negatively) in subsequent feedback, this group of students was able to formulate and embrace what they considered their duties and the division of labour as part of the course.

5. Assessment outcomes

Based on the students' enthusiasm for the course in general and for being in the driving seat, one might have expected that the assessment results would be remarkable too, e.g. that there would be no 2.2 or that there would be several first-class marks, and in the higher category. However, neither was the case. The results were reasonable but considering that the students had formulated – quite taxing – essay questions themselves, I would have expected them to connect their chosen texts to those questions in a more persuasive way. However, their discussions on paper did not go any further than what had been said in class, and that is unusual. No matter the teaching approach of the course, some students usually manage to surprise the reader through integrating further reading and putting their argument in a deeper way than was evident in those students' essays or exams. So the deeper learning which is ostensibly tested in such essay-based assessment formats was not evident or could not be evidenced.

Whilst it seems that the course had achieved learning in terms of social engagement and independent progress-making, measuring such progress turned out not to necessarily be amenable to purely paper-based assessment. Therefore, the assessment format needs changing. This would also satisfy the need to offer a wider breadth of assessment to increase inclusivity, particularly for students whose mental health issues can be made worse by the type of 'ruminative' thinking required in essay writing (cf. Watkins & Teasdale, 2001). The question to answer through further research will be whether an assessment format that is more aligned with the express and tacit learning outcomes would result in higher grades or better recognition of the students' efforts.

6. Conclusion

Further research should evaluate to what extent the process of students working as co-creators can be rewarded compared to detailed and in-depth work with the texts themselves, which is what has 'counted' so far. Honing students' expectations to be in the driving seat needs to be a cross-curricular activity, which requires peers to be comfortable with this, and a curriculum that emphasises independent learning. I would encourage colleagues to try students as partners, and experience them in a new light.

References

Brew, A. (2012). Teaching and research: new relationships and their implications for inquiry-based teaching and learning in higher education. *Higher Education Research and Development, 31*(1), 101-114. https://doi.org/10.1080/07294360.2012.642844

College of Arts and Law. (n.d.). *College of Arts and Law strategy 2015-2020*. University of Birmingham. https://intranet.birmingham.ac.uk/arts-law/documents/staff/sf/CAL-Strategy-2015-20.pdf

Dohm, H. (1917). *Der Missbrauch des Todes* [first publ. 1918]. Die Aktion. http://gutenberg.spiegel.de/buch/-4769/1

Ecojesuit. (2016). *Discarded life jackets in Lesbos need a waste management plan*. http://www.ecojesuit.com/discarded-life-jackets-in-lesbos-need-a-waste-management-plan/9230/

Healey, M. (2017). *Institutional and college strategies to engaging students as partners in research and enquiry*. University of Birmingham.

Healey, M., Flit, A., & Harrington, K. (2016). Students as partners: reflections on a conceptual framework. *Teaching and Learning Inquiry, 4*(2), 1-13. https://doi.org/10.20343/teachlearninqu.4.2.3

Healey, M., & Jenkins, A. (2009). *Developing undergraduate research and enquiry*. HEA. https://www.heacademy.ac.uk/knowledge-hub/developing-undergraduate-research-and-inquiry

Jenkins, A., & Healey, M. (2005). *Institutional strategies to link teaching and research*. HEA.

Suttner, B. von. (2005/1897). Gott verzeihe ihr. In D. Sudhoff (Ed.), *Erzählungen deutscher Schriftstellerinnen aus Böhmen und Mähren* (pp. 23-28). Arco Verlag.

Watkins, E., & Teasdale, J. D. (2001). Rumination and overgeneral memory in depression: effects of self-focus and analytical thinking. *Journal of Abnormal Psychology, 110*(2), 353-357. https://doi.org/10.1037/0021-843X.110.2.333

12 Beyond the language class

Mária Czellér[1] and Klára Nagy-Bodnár[2]

Abstract

As economies are inevitably becoming dominated by multinational and global companies, the need for Language for Specific Purposes (LSP) is growing accordingly. Language institutes in higher education are trying to tailor their curriculum to meet the expectations of such companies each with their specific technical vocabulary. While LSP courses are basically successful in providing graduates with the indispensable components of language competencies, the reality is that almost all such corporations have developed their own specific terminology, unfamiliar to LSP at large. This implies that the newly recruited employee is bound to be faced with the prospect of having to master technical jargon peculiar to the given corporate environment. The aim of the present paper is to demonstrate how the advantages of and skills in efficient – mostly digital – materials design on behalf of the teacher can be transferred to those having to continue developing vocabulary, communication, and interpersonal skills after the completion of formal training. The need for such methodology is justified by the findings of a survey recently conducted among young employees of multinational companies in a major city in Hungary.

Keywords: employability, transfer of materials design, language for specific purposes.

1. University of Debrecen, Debrecen, Hungary; czeller.maria@econ.unideb.hu

2. University of Debrecen, Debrecen, Hungary; bodnar.klara@econ.unideb.hu

How to cite this chapter: Czellér, M., & Nagy-Bodnár, K. (2019). Beyond the language class. In C. Goria, L. Guetta, N. Hughes, S. Reisenleutner & O. Speicher (Eds), *Professional competencies in language learning and teaching* (pp. 133-144). Research-publishing.net. https://doi.org/10.14705/rpnet.2019.34.921

Chapter 12

1. Introduction

Apart from the qualifications multinational and global companies require, the competitiveness of new graduates in the labour market is strongly influenced by the skills they possess. One of the crucial skills expected of professionals is foreign language proficiency, as it provides an advantage for those involved in the selection process and also for business organisations in their international activities (Hajdu & Czellér, 2016).

Accordingly, the European and particularly the Hungarian labour market has seen a dramatic increase in "[e]mployers' demands for highly qualified workforce with excellent communication skills and a decent command of one or more foreign languages [for the past decade]" (Czellér & Nagy-Bodnár, 2016, p. 75).

Having realised these requirements, language institutions in Hungarian higher education have been offering a wide range of English for Specific Purposes (ESP) and LSP courses incorporated in their curricula to prepare students to face the challenges the labour market presents.

LSP courses have proved to be successful in providing graduates with the general and indispensable components of language competencies including reading, technical vocabulary, oral communication, listening, writing, confidence in the use of grammar and the basics of intercultural skills. As a result, most graduates manage to land jobs with promising perspectives.

However, a new position at international companies tends to present specific language requirements well beyond the scope of ESP or LSP classes, thus well beyond the language teacher's control.

There is an old Chinese saying: 'Give a man a fish, he will eat for a night – teach a man how to fish, he'll never go hungry again'.

Owing to the nature of the technical language of different professional fields – particularly that of the business world – in line with the socio-economic environment and the diversity of corporate cultures, no LSP training course in formal education can fully ensure that the language learner will master the interpersonal skills and the specific vocabulary relevant to a given workplace. Companies tend to develop their own specific terminology, and the job-related vocabulary may be too specific to be included in any course book.

Newly recruited employees may find themselves at a loss even after years of studying the foreign language. Consequently, continuous progress in oral and written communication should be anticipated.

The objective of the present article is to demonstrate how language teachers can help young professionals overcome the above-mentioned obstacles. A possible solution to facilitate the new employee's individual language learning progress is to transfer to the students certain elements of materials design during the LSP courses. The paper intends to highlight one specific area of the application of digital resources and devices – the sophisticated word processor – as it is most suitable for individual study and, although indispensable in every aspect of our professional work, is still not fully exploited.

The shift in the application of computer platforms towards mobile devices – especially tablets and smartphones – coupled with the availability of pictures, sound, and video has overshadowed the potentials of the word processor, which is also available online.

The concept of life-long learning is both necessitated by today's society and globalised economies, and facilitated by digital mobile devices and Internet-based resources.

2. Method

The need for skills transfer has become obvious from a survey carried out among employees of multinational corporations in Debrecen, a major city in the northeast of Hungary. The objective of the survey was to make an assessment of the adaptability and degree of usefulness of language skills acquired in LSP courses at the University of Debrecen and in some other institutions of higher education, mainly in the eastern part of the country.

Young professionals were asked to fill in a questionnaire and semi formal interviews were also conducted. Although much of the information gained was predictable and the findings merely helped confirm certain assumptions, the responses shed light on some intricate, less obvious factors as well.

3. Results

Some questions most relevant to the topic of the paper are discussed below.

Question 1. How important was your command of a foreign language in landing your current job?

On a scale from one, meaning not important at all, to five, representing absolutely essential, the answers averaged five. The maximum score to this basic question was in accord with expectations. Not surprisingly, all respondents agreed that they would not have been hired if they had lacked foreign language skills, irrespective of their qualifications.

Question 2. To what extent does your command of a foreign language correspond to the requirements of your current position?

The responses had an average score of 3.9. Taking into consideration the fact that all the participants in the survey had a good command of at least one foreign language, levels B2 or C1 according to the Common European Framework of Reference, – a B2-level certificate in at least one foreign language is the prerequisite for the issue of a degree in Hungary –, the score of 3.9 seems relatively low. It clearly shows that they have to continue developing their language knowledge and keep themselves up-to-date on a regular basis in order to be able to fulfil professional requirements.

Question 3. What language skills and competencies do you think you should develop further?

The respondents' answers suggest that the young employees' priorities include both general and technical vocabulary, with special emphasis on job-related terminology (see Figure 1).

Figure 1. Answers to Question 3 (a: speaking, b: listening, c: reading, d: writing, e: general vocabulary, f: technical vocabulary, g: grammar, h: translation, i: presentation)

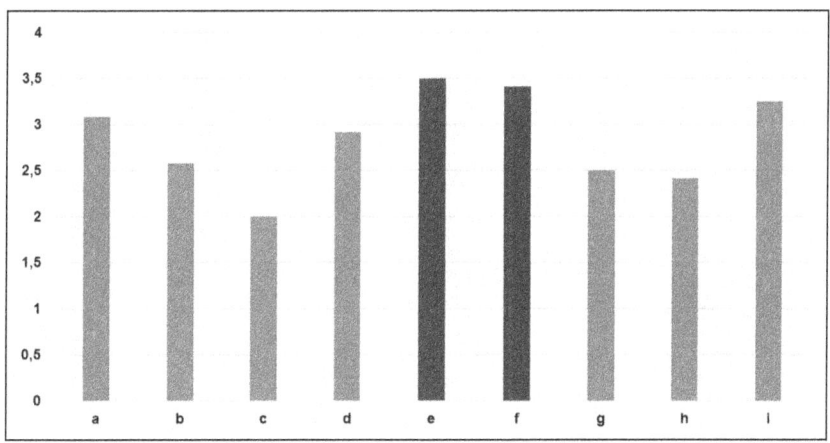

Question 5. How do you improve your English on your own?

With the advent of the digital era, both the learner and the teacher have become receptive to novel ways of language acquisition over the past two decades. In the absence of formal training, young professionals tend to show a preference for the vast amount of digital resources as opposed to printed ones (coursebooks, newspapers) available for individual work (Figure 2). Efficiency in self-study, however, cannot be taken for granted as a result of the availability of resources; it can only be achieved relying on an optimal approach incorporating both human and technical factors. The learner has to be prepared for this phase of individual study prior to graduation, during their studies at university or college, when the language teacher still has the opportunity to transfer certain techniques, elements of materials design, to students in order to facilitate the individual learning process.

Figure 2. Answers to Question 5 (a: course books, b: radio/TV, c: reading articles on the net, d: language courses on the net, e: videos (Youtube, etc.), f: websites with professional content)

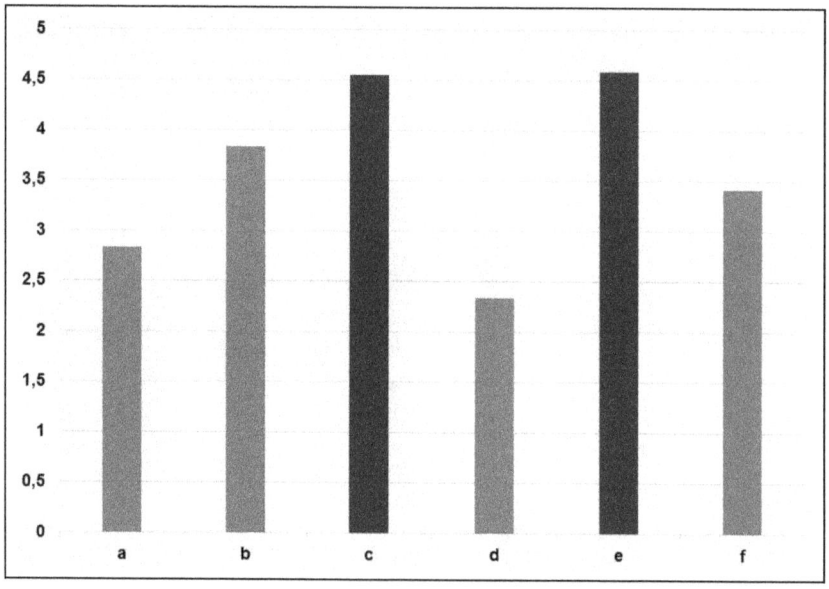

The application of up-to-date digital resources may require thoughtful consideration and even restraint. When the students use online resources, the teacher should give exact methodological guidelines on how to use them, browsing the net should always be task based (Czellér & Nagy-Bodnár, 2018).

As a result of the introduction of commercially available computers (ZX Spectrum, Commodore 64) in the early 1980's, foreign language teaching became one of the areas trying to exploit the potentials of the new technology. The first attempts resulted in simple programmes created by computer specialists. The methodology was in its infancy, the creation of such digital materials relied on the computer programmer, and language teachers were unable to create their own programmes.

The spread of the IBM compatible Personal Computers (PCs) in the late 1980's and 1990's together with word processors represented a breakthrough in the application of computers for language teachers. It was at that time that the language teacher became truly involved in the use of computers for language teaching purposes. The process of test-creation, editing, correction, and storage etc. became a fundamentally simple task for the teacher.

The 1990's also saw the introduction of object-oriented programming languages and Windows-based programmes. Multimedia applications on CDs and online language teaching programmes have been released aiming to facilitate all aspects of language acquisition including basic skills such as reading, listening, and even writing and speaking.

Over the past decade, the Internet, social media, speech recognition, speech synthesis, and artificial intelligence have been in the forefront. The level of sophistication of groundbreaking innovations in the digital world – virtual reality, robotics, Youtube etc. – has once again overshadowed the fine-tuned potentials of the word processor, which, however, can be equally useful for the language learner.

The past decades have seen a shifting focus from the computer programmer (+ language teacher) towards the language teacher (+ computer programmer), through the emergence of online resources to the learner. It seems appropriate for language learners to utilise some of the possibilities in such a way that they develop a more creative and analytical approach to them. A dynamic and ambitious attitude is a precondition for life-long learning and elements of materials design in language acquisition seem compatible with it. As Gündüz (2005) states,

> "[t]he language laboratories [created in the 1970's gave way] to computer assisted language learning work stations. 'Micro computers

Chapter 12

used as word processors complement the audio facilities, enabling the interactive teaching of all four language skills reading, listening, speaking and writing'. (Crystal, 1987, p. 377). Crystal further adds that today a great variety of [foreign language teaching] exercises, such as sentence restructuring, checking of spelling, checking of translations, or dictation tasks, and cloze tests can be computationally controlled using texts displayed on the screen" (p. 194).

While back in 1987 Crystal mentioned the usefulness of 'text displayed on screen', three decades later it is equally important to examine the methods with which texts can be organically incorporated into language development. This method implies an approach that is analytical, creative, and is in the form of self-study.

As progress is a never-ending phenomenon and the framework of language teaching in the distant future cannot be predicted, currently, the main concern of language learners should be the maximum degree of exploitation of the existing possibilities. Therefore, the importance of the potential advantages of the fine-tuned word-processor has to be emphasised, with the help of which useful tasks such as analytical reading can be performed.

One objective of analytical reading is to sensitise learners to even minute details relating to grammar, vocabulary, collocations, idiomatic language, style, register, and syntax. The method lies in the notion that, instead of presenting rules and giving exercises to students for practising and drilling, which are common components of the traditional methodology of language teaching, the teacher should encourage the student to find, discover, and reveal the same aspects of the language by carrying out simple research into the text, the possibility of which is offered by the latest versions of word processing programmes, the most common of which is Microsoft Word.

Since the new file format 'docx' was introduced, Microsoft Word has incorporated a number of useful improvements which are only comparable to functions of concordance programmes. Statistical data concerning frequency of occurrence, textual environment, for example, hitherto exploited by linguists and literary scholars, are now available to any language learner. The most notable of these features is the 'find' command, which can be successfully used for analytical reading.

One of the most trivial statements made in connection with language development – be it the speaker's mother tongue or a foreign language – is that reading is one of the most basic and also the most useful means of fostering and promoting verbal expression. Although the advantages of reading are undeniable, today's technologically sophisticated world has altered the present generation's attitude to reading in such a way that the availability of information has shifted the interest in detail towards a focus on reading in the form of scanning or skimming a great number of texts with the maximum speed. The tendency and capability to sort out the main points of a text, while an ultimately considerable skill, is bound to decrease awareness of details of a foreign language which are still essential components of language development.

As a result of the widespread application of the communicative approach, and English being a lingua franca, a common means of communication between speakers of different languages, students feel empowered to interact freely and creatively.

Another consequence of this teaching method is a certain degree of permissiveness on behalf of the teacher in terms of choice of vocabulary, grammar, and pronunciation for the sake of the student's fluency, self-confidence, and an optimal degree of spontaneity.

In order to facilitate the correct use of a foreign language, the teacher has to find novel ways of making students more sensitive to such details and making them internalise the correct forms for themselves. One useful tool to achieve this goal is to give project-like tasks to students basically as homework, which leads to discovering particular lexical or grammatical features of a language. Providing the student with text-based authentic examples for home study is likely to be beneficial. Recommended steps are as follows:

- the teacher selects useful (mostly online) resources and texts;

- the link of the text is sent to the students for home study; and

- the student's task is to use the 'search' function of the word processor (Ctrl+F) for particular features of the language. The occurrences of words, phrases or grammar items in the given text will be automatically listed and highlighted.

The example that follows illustrates how this simple method can be used: for instance grammar – singular or plural. Table 1 shows the correct use of English non-count nouns (e.g. news, information, advice, furniture, equipment, etc.). Despite being aware of the grammatical rule, students tend to use such words incorrectly (either with the indefinite article or in the plural). With the help of the 'find' command, the student is given instant examples of how such words are used in a text and the authentic, real-life occurrences may reinforce and activate existing passive vocabulary and knowledge of grammar.

Table 1. Travel safety[3]

Navigation	Non-count nouns: e.g. advice
• The FCO travel advice helps you • provide tailored advice for • you should read the travel advice • on the travel advice page	"The FCO travel advice helps you make your own decisions about foreign travel. Your safety is our main concern, but we can't provide tailored advice for individual trips. If you're concerned about whether or not it's safe for you to travel, you should read the travel advice for the country or territory you're travelling to, together with information from other sources you've identified, before making your own decision on whether to travel. Only you can decide whether it's safe for you to travel. When we judge the level of risk to British nationals in a particular place has become unacceptably high, we'll state on the travel advice page for that country or territory that we advise against all or all but essential travel. Read more about how the FCO assesses and categorises risk in foreign travel advice. Our crisis overseas page suggests additional things you can do before and during foreign travel to help you stay safe".

3. https://www.gov.uk/foreign-travel-advice/hungary/contact-fco-travel-advice-team

Despite its simplicity, this process of listing and highlighting can considerably contribute to the clarification of other problematic areas of English grammar.

4. Conclusion

Regular application of the method described above can enable the student to exploit these features of the word processor and benefit from it in the same way as they are prepared to use online dictionaries. Nonetheless, as Dhaif (1989) says,

> "computers can never replace the 'live' teacher, especially in language teaching, where the emphasis is on mutual communication between people. [Computers] can just play a role in teaching the second or foreign language as an aid to the teacher" (cited in Razagifard & Rahimpour, 2010, p.11).

While this claim may hold true for the foreseeable future, the role of the teacher is bound to undergo considerable transformation as a result of artificial intelligence, which is gradually pervading all aspects of our intellectual life.

References

Crystal, D. (1987). *The Cambridge encyclopedia of the English language.* Cambridge University Press.

Czellér, M., & Nagy-Bodnár, K. (2016). Preparing students for business language examination with special emphasis on developing speaking skills. *Journal of Languages for Specific Purposes, 2016,* 73-81. http://jlsp.steconomiceuoradea.ro/wp-content/uploads/2016/03/jlsp-3-martie-2016.pdf?

Czellér, M., & Nagy-Bodnár, K. (2018). Tourism in focus: teaching ESP for students majoring in tourism and hospitality. In *Teaching English for specific purposes at universities.* Brno University of Technology, Faculty of Electrical Engineering and Communication.

Dhaif, H. A. (1989). Can computers teach languages? *English teaching forum, 27*(3), 17-19.

Gündüz, N. (2005). Computer assisted language learning. *Journal of Language and linguistic studies, 1*(2), 193-214.

Hajdu, Z., & Czellér, M. (2016). Adapting language education to the expectations of the labour market. In N. Gajšt, A. Plos & P. Vičič (Eds), *The ninth international language conference on the importance of learning professional foreign languages for communication between cultures* (pp. 63-67). Ekonomska- poslovna fakulteta Univerze v Mariboru.

Razagifard, P., & Rahimpour, M. (2010). The effect of computer-mediated corrective feedback on the development of second language learners' grammar. *International Journal of Instructional Technology and Distance Learning, 7*(5), 11-29. http://www.itdl.org/Journal/May_10/May_10.pdf?

Author index

A
Andrés, Chelo de vii, 6, 99

B
Brick, Billy vii, 2, 19

C
Cervi-Wilson, Tiziana ix, 2, 19
Cunico, Sonia vii, 5, 53
Czellér, Mária ix, 7, 133

D
De Berg, Anna viii, 7, 111
Domonyi, Renáta x, 5, 65

G
Ghannam, Jumana viii, 4, 31
Goria, Cecilia v, 1
Guetta, Lea v, 1

H
Hajdu, Zita x, 5, 65
Hughes, Neil v, 1

J
Jordano de la Torre, María x, 4, 41

L
Lázár, Tímea x, 5, 77

M
Minoia, Marilena viii, 6, 89

N
Nagy-Bodnár, Klára xi, 7, 133

R
Reisenleutner, Sandra v, 1

S
Speicher, Oranna vi, 1

T
Tar, Ildikó xi, 5, 77

W
Webster-Deakin, Tara ix, 2, 9
Whittle, Ruth ix, 7, 121

www.ingramcontent.com/pod-product-compliance
Lightning Source LLC
Chambersburg PA
CBHW031631160426
43196CB00006B/373